THE SELF IN EDUCATION

The Self in Education

J.B. Thomas

NFER Publishing Company

For BETSI and AMY

Published by the NFER Publishing Company Ltd.,
Darville House, 2 Oxford Road East,
Windsor, Berks. SL4 1DF
Registered Office: The Mere, Upton Park, Slough, Berks. SL1 2DQ
First published 1980

ISBN 0 85633 212 7

Typeset by King, Thorne & Stace Ltd., School Road, Hove, Sussex BN3 5JE
Printed in Great Britain by
Page Bros (Norwich) Ltd
Distributed in the USA by Humanities Press Inc.,
Atlantic Highlands, New Jersey 07716 USA

Contents

Acknowledgements

It is six years since the NFER Publishing Company Limited produced my bibliographical guide to self-concept studies in psychology and education and I am grateful for its invitation to write this brief introduction to the study of self-concept. Special thanks must go to J.K. Sansom, Enver Carim and Veda Dovaston for their encouragement and editorial advice. Thanks are also due to the Editors of the Durham Research Review for permission to rework material from two papers published in that journal, to my friends and colleagues Louis Cohen, Philip Lanch and Cyril Simmons for helpful comments on the manuscript at various stages, to Angela Fairmann for the patient typing of awful handwriting, and to Mona McKay for her expert librarianship. Finally I must thank my wife Betsi for her careful reading of the manuscript and assistance in preparing the bibliography. Any faults of commission or omission in the completed text are the responsibility of the author alone.

Foreword

The study of self-concept has become increasingly popular with writers on education in the last decade and the subject evokes enthusiasm in students and teachers. These students and teachers lack a brief British introduction to self-concept in book form, though very readable chapters exist in isolated collections of previously published papers or as discrete parts of publications devoted to larger topics. I have tried to meet the need for such a text and have written it in the form of four critical surveys of the literature (Chapters 3 to 6) against a background of issues in methods and theory (Chapters 1 and 2). It will be obvious that the material available is very unevenly spread, and that some aspects of self-concept have received much more sustained scholarly coverage by researchers than others. I have tried to strike a balance in this 'state of the art' review by selecting some studies for more detailed comment out of what must needs be a broad and selective survey. The text is aimed at undergraduate and postgraduate students of education, and at those students or teachers who may wish to pursue their own research in this area or gain a rapid overview of studies in the field as part of their work for advanced qualifications in teaching.

J.B. Thomas
Loughborough University

Chapter 1

Methods and Measurement

'Self-concept – who an individual thinks he is and the unique traits he believes himself to possess – is the core of virtually all issues in social psychology.' This quotation from Webster and Sobieszek (1974) reveals the centrality and importance of the theories and studies to be examined in this book. The self concept is the core of many issues in areas other than social behaviour; it is of the utmost importance in educational and clinical settings. Indeed the literature of self-concept is drawn from many disciplines – philosophy, psychology, sociology, psychiatry and anthropology. The centrality of the concept and the rapid growth of the literature is the justification for this chapter. This book must by its nature be selective and no one study can be treated in sufficient depth. Introductory texts in education and psychology often cover the self with no mention of the methodological problems involved in their broad generalized statements of research findings. It is therefore the purpose of this chapter to introduce the reader to some of the methods used, to indicate sources of research instruments, and to show the difficulties and pitfalls in self-concept measurement. The chapter is therefore somewhat technical and readers willing to take the rest of this book on trust may start at Chapter 2, and return to this chapter when they have completed their reading. Buyer beware, however! Problems of method often arise from problems of definition and theory and Chapters 1 and 2 complement each other before we turn to the literature reviews which are the major concern of the author.

Methods of Study

Most of the research techniques used in self-concept research were not specially designed for it, many studies are descriptive rather than explanatory, the self is often unrealistically treated as if developments in it occur in isolation from developments in other areas (e.g. intelligence), information is often inferred not directly observed, and the researchers may have a theoretical bias which is not obvious on reading their findings. These general caveats must be remembered as we review methods of study. More specific psychometric problems will be handled later. In this section we look at the individual case study, qualitative data, cross-sectional studies, longitudinal approaches, and conclude with the different techniques used to produce data for various statistical treatments. Much of our comment is true of child and educational psychology in general and we are still feeling our way in a young science for not until the twentieth century did we have a real growth of developmental psychology as general psychology developed.

The individual case study of one child or adolescent where the social, psychological, medical, environmental, biographical and other information available about a person is used to explain or illustrate his or her view of self has not been much used in self-concept study. Statistically minded writers would regard it as 'soft' data though it is used extensively by psychologists and psychiatrists (e.g. Laing, 1961) to supplement other findings, to give valuable insights into the practical implications of various theories of self development, and as a necessary tool in diagnosis and treatment of psychopathology. The study of human behaviour is much more than the aggregate of countless case studies though, however interesting, and Laing warns us against too individual an approach: 'even an account of one person cannot afford to forget that each person is always acting upon others and acted upon by others. No one acts or experiences in a vacuum. The person whom we describe and over whom we theorize is not the only agent in his world'. In addition to Laing's structure two further points must be kept in mind about case studies. It would be foolhardy to generalize from findings on one person to describing self-concept growth or behaviour in a group, and, especially with children, incautious to predict future behaviour from present and often incomplete observations. Nevertheless the case study technique can be a rich and fruitful source of information on the self, as demonstrated with great skill by Axline (1971) in her classic 'Dibs: in Search of Self', an account of play therapy and applied psychoanalytical theory in the successful treatment of a bizarre, withdrawn, and highly intelligent six year old. Axline shows the true value of case study material, the provision of in-depth data to illustrate a theoretical position or to give concrete evidence of a psychological construct operating in an individual experience. There is room for more case study approaches in the psychological study of self, and for the intelligent and perceptive use of historical, autobiographical and literary data, along the lines of Erikson's 'Young Man Luther' or the use of work by Genet and Dostoyevsky put to good effect by Laing (1961) in 'Self and Others'. Obviously in such work one must appreciate the peculiar historical and critical problems involved but much of value to the self theorist could be obtained by applying psychological techniques to such work as Simone de Beauvoir's 'Memoirs of a Dutiful Daughter' or 'The Diary of Anne Frank'. We have useful models in Freud's 'A Young Girl's Diary' and psychological precedent in the use of literary and introspective materials in creativity research.

Approaches such as those mentioned in the last paragraph are qualitative data, information not collected or presented in a quantitative form but which, where possible, may be analysed or categorized in ways which permit statistical treatment and publication in tabulated form. Apart from case study materials, the self concept has been investigated through the use of diaries and compositions. Sometimes these form the sole source of information. At other times they are the basis for a more sophisticated methodology. Essentially the rationale behind the approach is based on psychoanalytical theory, refers more to a school of thought than to a specific method, and is associated with the writings of Freud, Jung, Adler and other theories and therapies derived from psychoanalysis. The basic belief is that behaviour is explained through unconscious processes entering conscious behaviour in various ways, e.g. in speech, letters, diaries, drawings, craft work and doll-play. It must be added that the psychoanalytical approach underlies much of the psychometric research. In any case the credence one places on qualitative data will often depend on one's faith in unconscious processes and in projective techniques of investigation. Evaluation of the work of Axline depends on the reader appreciating its Freudian approach (though not a rigid approach, for Axline appears influenced also by the work of Carl Rogers).

Essays and compositions have been used by many writers on self-concept, including influential studies by Jersild (1952) and Strang (1957). Crow (1962) published excerpts from the diary of a teenage girl and Emmett (1959) contains interesting and insightful essay material from pupils in a secondary modern school. Some studies have added depth to statistical data through using illustrative children's compositions (Thomas, 1974) though often the compositions have not been quoted in the published research, as is the case with Olasehinde (1972). The usual methodological approach with essay data is content analysis sentence by sentence for statements, phrases or adjectives descriptive of the self. These descriptions are then classified into categories revealed in the material and not into categories presupposed by the writer. This follows the design adopted by Havighurst and MacDonald (1955) and other writers quoted in this paragraph.

Composition data of this type is difficult to validate for various reasons, not the least being that the less able pupil writes far less and produces more irrelevant material than the able child and is relatively unable to articulate his stimulus field and his response to it. However, there is little reason to believe that compositions on self written by older children and adolescents are dishonest. By the age of ten or twelve the individual appears to have sufficient experience and ability to begin to think abstractly, so that he can make general assessments of his qualities and abilities. It could be argued that the social desirability factor is less likely to produce false responses in young children (Warburton, 1962) and as Zahran (1967) comments, the distorting effects of social desirability are not as great as often emphasized in self-rating techniques, and probably only holders of extremely negative self-concepts will distort responses. Anastasi (1968) has also claimed that self-report instruments are actually measures of self-concept. As a composition is a self-report instrument such data may be said to be valid. One should not, though, be complacent about problems of reliability and validity arising from qualitative data and that, unless one uses very large samples, such data is difficult to generalize from and difficult to synthesize. Nevertheless essays, diaries, and related materials illustrate the determinants of self-concept: home, school, and peer influences. The materials reflect the values of the adult influencing the child and adolescent, show age and sex differences, and indicate the important relationship between physical development and the growth of self-concept in the child. Analysis also informs us about the structure of self-concept and relate to Jersild's categories of physical characteristics, health, material possessions, personal relationships, school, intellectual status, social attitudes and other traits (Jersild, 1952). The perceptions of the writer in qualitative data may be faulty but they are real enough to him and reflect the person he thinks he is, his transitory self in time, his social self as others see him, and the ideal self he hopes to be. From the point of view of making research more acceptable to the teacher, they put human flesh on the psychometric bones and go some way to lessening any alienation between the researcher and the schools.

Insofar as self-concept development is seen as part of child development, there is one technique characteristic of (though not unique to) child development which has been used to some extent in self-concept research, but deserves to be used more widely. This is the longitudinal approach or research method where the same group of subjects is studied, tested and observed repeatedly over an extended period of time. The adoption of this approach makes it possible to study the development of a single person, and to investigate changes in self-concept both individually and in groups. Engel (1959) is one of the best know longitudinal studies of self-concept. Longitudinal researches, also called follow-up studies, make possible an investigation of relationships between different growth processes, and are among the most valuable in modern child and adolescent psychology, partly because of the known fallibility of any single testing or assessment of self-concept and variation in a child at any given point of time. As Professor Ronald Davie (1972) has pointed out the approach is not exclusive to the research worker and a school-based system of continuous assessment, for example, is longitudinal in nature and designed to monitor individual or group development. The same writer points out the essential strength of the method: 'the fact that the present results are seen in the context of what has been recorded before for each child. The total picture reflects the dynamic nature of the individual child's development'. The longitudinal approach does throw up serious problems which explain its limited use in self-concept research. It is most successful where team-work is involved and where research is carefully planned and funded. Such conditions are rare in self-concept study. Longitudinal studies, to be of the greatest use, must continue research over a long period of time, sometimes many years. This is not only costly of time and personnel, one is likely to lose contact for various reasons with one's subjects, or even have many changes in the research team. One of the most famous longitudinal studies, Terman's 'Genetic Studies of Genius' required the services of several researchers over the decades of investigation. A further disadvantage of the longitudinal approach is that we know little about how repeated exposure to psychological investigation affects the subjects in such studies.

Largely because of these problems of cost and time the student of self-concept is more likely to read cross-sectional studies, where tests or other measures of self-concept would be given all at once to children of different ages, i.e. to groups of ten-year-olds, eleven-year-olds, twelve-year-olds and so on. Comparison of data obtained at these different age levels would enable the researcher to describe age-trends in self-concept development. In short, age changes may be studied by longitudinal or cross-sectional methods, but an important disadvantage occurs in the latter approach, for, as Williams (1977) reminds us: 'the cross-sectional study very often masks great variations in the development of individuals'. In studies of body concept, for example, the growth of early and late physical developers is masked in the cross-sectional study which smooths out rapid growth rates. The study of individual trends must be longitudinal for it requires repeated testing. It must also be said of cross-sectional approaches that our statements of development of self-concept from, say, age twelve through to eighteen are inferred, because our group of twelve-year-olds are not the persons we investigate at eighteen. They are a different group examined at the same time as our twelve-year-olds and we infer that the latter will exhibit the characteristics of eighteen-year-olds when they themselves are eighteen years old, six years later. Historical and other situational changes may, of course, produce very different eighteen-year-old adolescents.

A particular type of longitudinal study with its own peculiar advantages and disadvantages is the retrospective study where an examination of self-concept at the present time may be preceded by inquiries about previous experience aimed at explaining their present development. This is cheaper and quicker than the normal longitudinal study and avoids the problems of cross-sectional research mentioned above. Retrospective studies face many of the practical difficulties of the case study approach as people's memories are fallible and their perception of past events selective. Relevant recorded information may be incomplete or inaccurate and, more seriously, retrospective recall may be influenced by the informants knowledge of subsequent events. Thus if a child has present difficulties his parents, friends or teachers are more likely to remember earlier problems, or events which they (perhaps wrongly?) assume to be relevant. Parents of children with no anxieties may remember no significant earlier events. In both sets of parents and their children the sequence of events may be confused and some events, as we know from Bartlett's work on constructive remembering, may never even have occurred. A further shortcoming of the approach is that it is very rare to find an invariable or consistent association between an earlier event and some later situation. Thus, although a group of children from broken homes may show problems of self-rejection, it does not automatically follow that all will do so. The faults noted here should be looked for in any clinical studies of self-concept (e.g. Axline, 1971) or in any work where information has not been directly obtained by the investigator, e.g. when reliance is placed on records of past health, school attainment, and so on.

The methods so far investigated are largely descriptive and however refined they can become in practice they do not allow us to make causal inferences or test hypotheses. We may note that a change of teacher leads to a more positive academic self-concept, for example, but we cannot conclude that the latter is necessarily caused by the former. In order to do this, we need to design experiments. The experimental approach of the psychologists is clearly and concisely outlined by Williams (1977) as follows: an experiment 'allows us to intervene in development in controlled ways so that we can assess the result of our intervention and then, hopefully, make sounder inferences about the causal relationships between the experiences which children have had and their development. The central features of the experiments which psychologists set up lie in the control exercised by the experimenter over the experiences which the children will receive. In ideal circumstances, one variable at a time is changed in the experimental situation, and given acceptable methods of assigning groups of children to different treatment conditions, safe inferences can be made'. Thus children may be matched in pairs or in groups for study and much self-concept research uses such methods involving controlled, pre-arranged intervention or manipulation by the experimenter. The experimental method has one major drawback, however, in that it can sometimes become so removed from the realities of human experience that its carefully arrived at results may be, and sometimes are, contrary to common sense or psychological observation. When this happens one should not dismiss the experimental approach out of hand but look for faults in the experimental design and in the administration of any testing instruments.

Testing instruments may be used in any of the approaches so far discussed, but the bulk of self-concept literature is based on psychometric research, that is, on results of the statistical treatment of self-concept measures given to subjects in or not in an experimental situation. Writers of psychometric studies of self-concept must obey basic rules of the game and it is up to the reader to check that these rules are kept. These rules are so often broken that we consider their weaknesses in greater detail below under the heading 'difficulties of measurement'. Here we simply look at what should happen before moving on to examine the sources of self-concept test instruments. Researchers and readers of research papers need to pay specific attention to the date of any test used, the age range(s) for which any test may be used, the sources in which the measure is mentioned and the studies in which it has been used, the availability of the test, the description of the measure including the time taken for its administration, the sample sizes of tested groups, and whether one regards published norms and information on validity and reliability as satisfactory. Having chosen his test a writer must plan and record in a systematic way and control satisfactorily for validity and reliability, as indicated by Wylie (1974). Further, as Cohen (1976) states, a satisfactory report of such a study should show unambiguously what purpose the inquiry served and whether the research design and the adopted statistical treatment were appropriate to the purposes of the inquiry. It should be noted that psychometric measures vary greatly and we cannot cover all of them. Their variety is obvious from our next section and one should always ask whether the instrument or method used to obtain psychometric data is the most appropriate for any particular study. For example, repertory grid techniques are held to be less inaccurate or misleading than self-report methods. In its original form (Kelly, 1955), the repertory grid test asked a person to consider twenty people in groups of three at a time, and to state how two of them differed from the third. The responses express ways of classifying individuals and are called 'constructs'. The main attraction of this method is that the 'constructs' are provided by the subject himself, and not predetermined by the tester. However, as we have seen, qualitative data also may have this advantage. Another technique becoming popular in self-concept research is the semantic differential. When looking at studies using this latter approach one should remember the general principle that a technique derived from other than self theory may be applied uncritically in self-concept investigations. The general semantic differential approach of Osgood *et al.* (1957) to the measurement of meaning does not necessarily produce the most appropriate sets of adjectives for use in describing or examining the concept of 'self'. In this case technical improvements in test presentation as suggested by McNamara (1971) and Orpen (1972) may lead to apparent research progress but leave unconsidered the theoretical justifications to using the instrument in the first place.

Sources of Research Instruments

The researcher in self-concept who decides on psychometric approaches will have limits on the type of research he is able to carry out. There will be restrictions on time, finances, the training of himself or others in the use of tests, accessability to and types of subjects, physical facilities, and other constraints. Such restrictions will often determine the type of measure to be used with any group of subjects, and the use of well-established instruments rather than one of his own design is preferred. Research literature is often less than helpful to the newcomer in the field, often omitting such basic information as validity and reliability of the test used, and it is therefore valuable to have available various manuals of methodology in educational research. Manuals which are particularly useful for the student are Cohen (1976), Johnson (1976), Walker (1973), and, because of its sole concentration on the self-concept, especially Wylie (1974). Also useful are methodological papers such as Purkey (1968) and any attempts at improving existing methodology and which report important developments in the use of existing measures and instruments. An excellent example of the latter type of study is Bagley and Mallick (1978) which produces a useful short version of the Piers-Harris Self-Concept Scale. Wells and Marwell (1976) should be consulted for discussion of the measurement of self-esteem. The same authors make the valuable point that in the whole field of self-referent behaviour complex issues in the philosophy of science are involved as well as those problems of a more methodological or technical nature. This book is too limited to go into such issues but they should not be ignored.

Cohen (1976) is a manual of materials and methods for use by the educational researcher in classroom and schools. The self-concept section of the book reports various techniques of measurement and examines sixteen measures in all, including the 'Who Are You' technique (Kuhn and McPartland, 1954), self-concept of identity scales, the adjectival scale used by Lipsitt (1958), measures of self-esteem, self-image of academic ability, adjective generation, semantic differential. The work reported can be adapted for use in infant, primary, secondary and higher education. The book should be used cautiously, however, as the strengths and weaknesses of certain approaches can sometimes only be judged by tracing back to the original sources, all of which are carefully acknowledged.

The two-volume Johnson work is a valuable review of child development tests and measurements not generally available, and sixty pages are devoted to the study of self-concept. Earlier tests covering the period 1956–65 may be found in Johnson and Bommarito (1971). The Johnson volumes accumulate a great deal of instrumental data on measures concerned with different aspects of the structure of the self-concept, such as body image, academic ability, or ideal self, and other instruments deal with the child's self-concept in various roles, such as that of student. The reader is directed to various sources of information on specific tests. Students of self-concept are advised to begin with published measures because, generally speaking, such instruments are more carefully designed and have more supportive scientific data in the way of norms and evidence on reliability and validity. Self-concept measures are evaluated in the accumulated works of the late Oscar Buros, the U.S. social scientist who over many years compiled the Mental Measurements Year Books used by educational and clinical psychologists and published by the Buros Institute of Mental Measurements. The books first appeared in 1938 and, for example, the Seventh Mental Measurements Year Book (Buros, 1972) provides information on 1,157 published tests and 12,539 references on the construction, use and validity of specific tests. As Johnson has pointed out, the book also includes original reviews of tests as well as excerpted journal reviews, a large bibliography of books on testing, and a directory of publishers. Tests in Print II (Buros, 1974) is also an essential reference book, as is the separate Mental Measurements Yearbook Monograph on personality. Obviously these massive reference works deal with much more than self-concept measures, but no serious writer on self-concept can afford to ignore them, and Wylie (1974) generously directs the reader to them where the Buros reviewer differs from her in his opinion of an instrument. Neither can the student of self ignore Measures of Self-Concept K-12, produced by the staff of the Instructional Objectives Exchange (1972), which provides measures of self-concept for use with pupils at primary, intermediate, and secondary levels. The measurement procedures include direct self-report, inferential self-report and observational indicators. Beatty (1969) includes a few self-concept measures, and the National Foundation for Educational Research in England and Wales (NFER 1973, 1976) publishes a register of questionnaires and attitude scales. Walker (1973) produces measures of emotional growth in pre-school and kindergarten children which include projective techniques, unobtrusive measures, and observational procedures. The book is a comprehensive guide to professionals who wish to study affective behaviour and experience in children aged from three to six years old.

Ruth Wylie, a distinguished self-concept researcher, has updated her important 1961 study and her review of methodological considerations and measuring instruments published in 1974 must now be regarded as the authoritative reference work in this area of study. Chapter 4 describes instruments in most common use and evaluates extant self-concept measures, and includes evaluation of such techniques as the use of Q-sorts and the semantic differential. Measures fully evaluated by Wylie include Bills Index of Adjustment and Values (BIAV), the Coopersmith Self-Esteem Inventory (SEI), the Piers–Harris Children's Self-Concept Scale (PH), the Tennessee Self-Concept Scale (TSCS), the Who Are You (WAY), Twenty Sentences Test (TST), and projective tests. Full references are given to studies in which these instruments are used and Wylie makes recommendations on the use of the instruments and ways in which they could be improved in terms of reliability and validity, and highlights those instruments worthy of further research and development, e.g. the Piers–Harris Children's Self-Concept Scale (PH) and those which reflect a very unsatisfactory state of research, e.g. the Tennessee Self-Concept Scale (TSCS) and the Coopersmith Self-Esteem Inventory (SEI). Interestingly, as well as their validation study of the PH, Bagley and Mallick (1978) report their intention to study the responses of a twelve-year-old population to the short version of the Coopersmith Self-Esteem Inventory. The great strength of the work by Wylie is her close attention to the methodological shortcomings of much of the existing self-concept literature and we now note her misgivings and recommendations.

Difficulties in Measurement

Wylie wrote her revised 1974 volume because of an 'explosive proliferation' of references since her original study of 1961. Its major fault is a neglect of British studies which also have increased in number (Thomas, 1973). Wylie's extensive bibliography of over 1,100 books and papers cites only ten (sic) British references. The same absence of British references is noticeable in other texts and empirical reviews, e.g. Samuels (1977). At a time when British work is on the increase it is important to consider carefully the methodological issues raised in the existing, largely American, literature. It is a depressing feature of Wylie's exhaustive work that the kinds of shortcomings she found in 1961 are essentially still there thirteen years later. There is still the production of instruments often used in a single piece of research with little or no information on test construction, reliability or validity. This makes generalization and synthesis of literature difficult and slows down theoretical and methodological progress in an already complex and not properly explored area of psychological study, an area made more difficult because of the self-disclosure required from subjects asked to respond to the psychological instruments involved. This latter complication is part of a much wider problem we face in educational research in an attempt to give it higher scientific standards and is very noticeable in the self-concept area. Wylie lists the most commonly occurring faults in self-concept research as follows. The method used in any piece of research is often so vague as to prevent interpretation and analysis and makes replication of the research impossible. This is unfortunate in a relatively new research area where well-known, standardized techniques are unavailable. There is a common use of measures with undemonstrated, inadequate, or totally unexplored construct validity. Construct validity is the essential form of validity in self-concept research because, by definition, the cognitions and attitudes of a person about himself are private and beyond direct observation by the investigator. In such research predictive or concurrent validity is insufficient demonstration of validity of the instrument. The experimental design of many studies is poor. Control groups are inadequate or insufficient and frequently no information is given about matching or randomizing of groups. In many studies the reader is unable to identify factors which may afford a different interpretation of findings. Contamination between independent and dependent variables is often brought about in research, for example, by the use of overlapping instruments. Johnson (1976) pointed out that many researchers combine self-concept instruments or use them in connection with tests of other attributes like attitude to school, and in such studies one must pay careful attention to the design and suitability of all the measures used in the research. Returning to Wylie, she has noted the overgeneralization of findings based either on artificial and brief experimentation or on findings of unclear statistical significance. In some studies, significance tests may be significant by chance alone. Most studies of self-concept, as mentioned earlier, have been one-shot exercises, with no replication or even cross-validation, in which some of the significant findings may arise from procedural and instrumental idiosyncracies which are theoretically irrelevant. Only confusion can result from synthesising results obtained from heterogeneous, unreplicated findings. In some research the use of population or sociological independent variables which have unknown relevance to psychological variables precludes clear psychological interpretation of the obtained associations. Finally, where deception techniques have been used, ethical problems arise about the psychological violation of a person's right to privacy and a further technical problem of whether individuals have faked responses or given socially desirable replies.

Wylie suggests that further and more successful research on self-concept depends on satisfactorily meeting three requirements:

1. Using and developing a small number of sound instruments of measurement;
2. Developing a rational programme of sophisticated instrument development, with well constructed item banks, improved formats, and more advanced statistical treatment;
3. The systematic control of situational variables in the design, application, and interpretation of tests.

Authors like Wylie and others critical of the present state of self-concept methodology recognize that the weaknesses indicated are not merely experimental or technological in nature. Problems of method are often produced by theoretical problems and the theoretical and methodological difficulties feed off one another. Self theories overlap with one another. No one theory has attracted sufficient empirical investigation and many such investigations are not informed by or addressed to any special theoretical position. Measurement is further confused by the vagueness and incompleteness of a theory, especially in the phenomenological area, where, for example, it is difficult to empirically test the theories of Carl Rogers although he implies that his ideas can be tested and, unlike some theorists, welcomes such testing.

Ambiguities and other problems of measurement hence arise from the problems involved in the definition and conceptualization of self. It is to definition and theories of self that we turn in Chapter 2.

Chapter 2

Theory and Practice in Teaching

Definition

This chapter attempts to define the concept of self, trace the history of self-concept study, and indicate its relevance for the teacher. To give the simplest definition: the self-concept is the image or picture the person has of himself, which has developed through childhood and adolescence under the formative influences of home, school, and social environment, and forms his behaviour. Not all writers would be happy at seeing the self as an 'extra causal agent that dwells in the person and somehow generates or causes behaviour in ways that are separable from the organism in which *it* resides' (Mischel, 1977) but the present writer does consider that the notion of self should be subject to experimental thinking and that such thinking cannot profitably occur until we are clear on definition. Unfortunately there is no easy definition, as we realize when we look at historical developments for the term 'self-concept' has many, often conflicting, definitions, as any psychological dictionary reveals. Drever (1964) defines it in terms of personality or ego and employs the word 'self' as a prefix twenty-one times while English and English (1958) in their comprehensive examination of psychological and psychoanalytical terms produce nearly one thousand combinations of self. The word 'ego' has similar problems of definition and an over zealous search for a definition would not tell us anything useful about real people in the real world, and the term 'self' was in wide, inconsistent usage in various disciplines during the nineteenth century. Different writers have used different definitions for purposes of their own investigations, but most authors stress the importance of social roles (and attempts by the individual to synthesize them) and the importance of the body image or 'the body as a psychological experience and the individual's feelings and attitudes towards his own body' as Fisher and Cleveland (1958) have defined it. The notion of self can also be seen first as process and then as structure. On the former level, as a descriptive process by which the person perceives his behaviour, both external and internal feelings, and on the level of structure the system of concepts available to the person in trying to define himself. Some psychologists like Gergen (1968) feel that we should talk not of the self-concept but the process of self-conception and a theory of multiple selves, on the argument that we present different selves in different social situations. Others confuse the terms 'ego' and 'self', distinguish between 'person' and 'self' and in the history of the subject several different aspects of meanings of self are revealed. Readers are referred to Vernon (1964) for a review of definition to that date and as Clark Hull wrote of conflicting psychologies of learning in 1935: 'one of the most striking things about psychological theory in general is the wide disagreement among individual psychologists'. Wide disagreements exist amongst self theorists today and it would be foolish to deny the justifiable reasons for such differences. Problems abound in both the theory and methodology of studying the self concept and conflicts of opinion and approach are not merely semantic and indeed sometimes arise from what might be termed boundary disputes between psychologists, sociologists, and philosophers, all of whom might claim justifiably to have made major contributions to self concept, and whose boundaries are well defended against those like Holland (1977) who are brave enough to attempt to cross them. Coming down off the theoretical fence, a useful definition for our present purposes might be that of Zahran (1967) who defines self-concept as follows: 'an organised, learned, cognitive, and unitary configuration of conscious perceptions, conceptions, and evaluations by the individual, of his self as he actually is (Perceived Self), as others are supposed to see him (Other Self), and as he would most like to be (Ideal Self)'. This definition underlines the function of the self-concept as a motivating, integrating, and organizing force in a person's experience and as such it is influential in the school situation. As a developmental concept and part of the personality of the child it is obviously included in both the theory and practice of teaching and learning in that personality differences affect teaching and learning, while the school situation itself will affect the development and evaluation of the self-concept in the individual. Staines (1958) has summarized the importance of the self-concept in learning and teaching as follows: the self is ubiquitous in classroom behaviour; the self is a major learning outcome of the classroom; the self develops according to the laws of learning; once developed the self becomes a factor in all subsequent learning; the self conditions all further learning of the self, and the self can be changed by controlled experience.

Importance

Students of education find self-concept important not only for professional reasons, but also for reasons of personal growth, while the psychologist is likely to find his model of human behaviour and experience incomplete without consideration of the self as a construct. We strive for individuality from the beginning of life, from when we are small and weak babies lacking in mobility and control, extremely dependent, and perceiving our world through senses governed by basic organic needs. Growing up not only involves growing physically in size and control but includes the acquiring of values, knowledge and rationality; it involves increasing awareness of our social acts with and towards others. In short, from a relatively early age we develop concepts of ourselves as persons and begin the process of developing self-consciousness and self-responsibility (Curtis and Mays, 1978). Though consistent to some extent, our self-image changes during the developmental process from childhood to adulthood. We are concerned with problems of self-identity both to understand our past experience and to have some understanding of our future potential as we realize problems of inner conflict or of conflict between self and society and that our concept of self, realistic or not, imposes restrictions and limitations on us as individuals in our attempts to enhance ourselves. The more accurate our perception of ourselves, in our physical and mental aspects, the greater the possibility of changing behaviour and experience in ways we desire for improving our social relationships or solving emotional difficulties (Kleinke, 1978). In talking of our difficult path to self-actualization, Maslow (1954) has written that 'satisfaction of the self-esteem need leads to feelings of self-confidence, worth, strength and capability and adequacy, of being useful and necessary in the world. But thwarting of these needs produces feelings of inferiority, of weakness, and of helplessness.'

Self-concept is important as a psychological construct. Allport argued that the concept of self was necessary if only to avoid regarding a concept like motivation as anything other than a collection of instincts and conditioned drives. Cattell similarly put the self-concept in an important place in his psychological system, as did Jung, Gardner Murphy and other personality theorists, notably Carl Rogers who argued in contradiction to crude Skinnerian behaviourism and technology that the subjective choice in an individual must never be threatened. Ira Gordon (1962) places self-concept as the central concern of the developmental psychologist and this evaluation alone stresses the importance of the self-concept in education for the teacher is face to face with the developing child and adolescent and they in turn face the developing teacher in various stages of growth as an adult. As Radley (1979) has outlined, the psychology of education has yet to really appreciate that education is a social enterprise (a relational activity), involving students and teachers at a practical and personal level. Knowledge, at one level, is both an expression of these human relationships and a structure for them. Questions of self-concept are thus essentially educational questions for general educational decisions must consider the connections between growing self-consciousness and experiences in classroom, lectures or seminars.

History

The importance of the self-concept for the educator, whether educational psychologist or teacher, has encouraged a number of empirical studies in the development of self-concept which have reinforced its relevance for teaching. The last twenty years has seen a greater tolerance by behaviourists for the concept of self and there is now a substantial body of behavioural studies dealing with various aspects of the self. In addition, of course, are the studies of sociologists, social psychologists, and psychiatrists of all theoretical persuasions. These studies are more clearly understood against the historical background to the self-concept in psychology and in education. The historical treatment here is necessarily brief and the reader interested in the history of psychology may consult Diggory (1965) or Gergen (1971) and read some of the writers mentioned in depth. Hamachek (1965) reprints useful papers on the self-concept in the fields of educational growth, teaching and learning.

Self began as a philosophical concern and philosophical interest in the self-concept still continues as the important papers in Mischel (1977) and Curtis and Mays (1978) testify. Historically, philosophers as famous as Descartes and Leibniz treated the self as part of the body-mind problem which has fascinated philosophers and psychologists since classical times concerning the distinction between the physical human body and some non-physical entity, e.g. soul, spirit, psyche, mind, and in much philosophical writing such as that of Socrates or, much nearer our own time, Kierkegaard, the treatment of subjectivity and self is closely tied up with doctrines of moral goodness and a view that all learning is basically learning about the self. Only what is personally appropriated from the curriculum of life itself is truly known. This model of man closely resembles the viewpoint of phenomenological psychologists. It is an interesting exercise in history and analysis of science to trace particular psychological theories to specific philosophical writings but we must satisfy ourselves with the general statement that philosophy has enriched the psychological study of the self and that overtly understandable psychological theories throw up major philosophical and ethical questions. The Cartesian notion of the 'I', the thinking, knowing, cognizing entity became one direct predecessor of the concept of self and as psychology evolved as a separate entity from philosophy at the end of the nineteenth century the self as a related concept moved with it. William James (1890) propounded the following constituents of the self: the material self, consisting of the individual's material possessions, including his body; the social self, or the recognition received from others; the spiritual self, the inner or subjective being; pure ego, the stream of thought which makes up the individual's sense of personal identity. William James was the turning point in bringing the self to the attention of psychologists, though the philosopher C.S. Pierce had actually studied the development of self-consciousness in children some twenty years earlier and had stressed the importance for self-awareness of the child recognizing his own body as causing changes in the objects around him and Wundt, who could be called the father of experimental psychology, had commented in 1889 that the kinesthetic sensations a child experiences from his muscles formed a 'consciousness of self'. Before James then some psychologists had looked at self-awareness in objective terms and his own long chapter in his 'Principles of Psychology' encouraged further psychological investigation. James had laid claim to self as a psychological construct but the behaviourism which characterized the psychology of the first half of the twentieth century reduced self to a psychological concept of little importance, a position not enhanced by the vague theorizing of Calkins (1915) who attempted to demonstrate that there was a self discoverable in every act of introspection. Not only must one recognize that defence mechanisms and self-deception so contaminate introspection as to give a distorted view of the self but one must realize that a psychological method as philosophical as introspection was anathema to behaviourist schools of thought in psychology.

The development of self-concept theory was to suffer such behaviourist attacks because self theory did not appear related to empirical facts, experimentation was lacking, and it did not conform to the behavioural model of scientific psychology. But, as Gergen (1971) has written 'the realisation that learning theories often ignored activities and events internal to the organism opened the door to further study of the self theory' and indeed the scientific study of perception by Gestalt psychologists benefited self theory when the Gestalt psychologists extended their domain from perception to personality theory, motivation and social psychology and this beneficial effect is reflected in the work of writers like Allport, Rogers, Snygg and Combs and Murphy. In general, however, the self was abandoned by academic psychology and became the subject of numerous sociological and psychoanalytical theorists, with relatively little cross-fertilization, partly because Freud had little formal training in academic psychology and little contact with psychologists. Furthermore the specialized terminology of the various psychoanalytic schools created failures of communication between psychoanalysts and psychologists to such an extent that perhaps it explains the relative failure of academic psychology to study self theory in that an antipathy to Freudian psychology has perhaps produced an antipathy to studying the self-concept.

Mead

Sociologists had no such antipathy, however, and were quick to recognize that certain aspects of human behaviour were not likely to be analysed in a meaningful way unless one referred to the consciousness of selves – one's own self and those selves of one's fellow beings. C.H. Cooley and G.H. Mead are the founding sociological giants of self theory with the former arguing that self and society were inseparable concepts and Mead in a wide variety of learned articles arguing that the self arose from social conditions. Miller (1973) in a fascinating study of Mead stresses the latter's debt to Cooley. Cooley was influenced by the economist Adam Smith's looking glass theory of the self which stressed that, in the economic world, the seller must look at himself from the point of view of the buyer and vice versa. Each must take the attitude of the other. Cooley's development of these ideas impressed Mead who recognized that our own individual behaviour is conditioned by the behaviour and attitudes of others, e.g. Mead saw play as instrumental in the development of the self-concept, for other players in games with rules help condition the social play of their companions. Mead (1934) in 'Mind, Self and Society' argued that the child has no self at birth and that its development depends on social experience and activity so that the self is a learned structure of attitudes, built up by the organization of the perceived self of others towards himself and towards one another in social acts and situations and by the organization of the generalized attitudes of the social group to which he belongs. Mead's theory of the self, often regarded only as social behaviourism, is part of his wider educational theory presented in such papers as 'The Relation of Play to Education' (1896) and reflects a social philosophy influenced strongly by his personal involvement in the Chicago school system and by the theory of ethics held by his close friend and colleague John Dewey. Thus sociological views of self arising from Mead's work have, like the psychological studies, a common parentage in philosophical writings, and, indeed an understanding of Mead's view of self is facilitated by reading his essays on philosophy and education presented by Petras (1968). Mead's contribution to self theory is an elaboration of what William James had called the social self and places a theoretical emphasis on social interaction. This approach has been distinguished by Kinch (1963) as stressing that the individual's conception of himself emerges from interaction with other individuals and groups in society and this self-conception, in turn, guides or influences the behaviour of that individual.

Depth Psychology

The first half of the present century was a period of system building for psychologists and sociologists and of the depth psychologists the works of Freud (1949), Adler (1930), Horney (1946) and Sullivan (1964) are most relevant to the student of self theory, while some like Bertocci (1945) and Snygg and Combs (1949) appeared to believe that an understanding of self was the key to open every psychological door. Freud's contributions to self theory were indirect rather than direct in his postulation of the related concepts of id, ego and superego, though it should be recognized that there were always divergent and mutually antagonistic strands in Freud's thought and many writers have never given the Freudian theory of ego development full recognition. This is hardly surprising in that in his early work he played up instincts and undermined the role of the ego. The total effect of Freud's integration of his theories with his clinical practice, however, was a new sophistication for ego psychology and the self theorist who neglects the writing of Freud will miss much of value and stimulation to further research (Loevinger, 1976). Adler, whom Freud dismissed as merely an 'ego psychologist', in his individual psychology came to believe that the over-riding impulse in motivation came from the creative self encouraged by the acceptance and encouragement of parents and immediate friends. He argued that man was self-determining, making his own personality out of his heredity and experience, and the creative self ensures that the result is dynamic and unique. He pointed out that parents could be over-indulgent and produce self centred and demanding children incapable of mature and reciprocal relationships. In terms of G.H. Mead, the social self will be underdeveloped and immature. Adler saw human beings as striving consciously for personal goals. Jung's association with Freud and Adler did not prevent him developing his own concepts of the self arrived at through his clinical observations and his comparative material from historical sources, religion, folklore and alchemy. Fordham (1971) has given us a clear account of the empirical foundations and theories of the self in Jung's work, including his view that the self includes the unconscious psyche and 'embraces and includes the ego'. The work of Jung on self includes contradictions and in what we have just said if the self is regarded as the whole psyche then the self cannot be observed as such, since the ego is contained in it as a part and is therefore unable to act as a conscious observer. However the writings of Jung are stimulating for any self theorist and Fordham sees clear theoretical advantages in treating the self as a whole organism where room is left for the personal life of the individual and his relation to the external world as a whole. The major contribution of Karen Horney (1946) to the study of self-concept is her discussion of the consequences of and defences against feelings and experiences of anxiety. She stressed the danger of an unrealistic self-image where, extremely, the individual may convince himself of his own superiority or, realizing the differences between himself and his idealized image, submit himself to extreme disparagement. In contrast to genuine ideals, such an image has no dynamic quality and hinders the growth of a realistic self-concept because it prevents an acknowledgement of real shortcomings or inhibits attempts at overcoming them. Most of the work of Harry Stack Sullivan was published after his death and much of it was unformalized, but like Horney he examined the relationship between anxiety and the self system. In his paper 'Beginnings of the Self System' (1964) the self system is formulated as an internal organization of controls evolved from man's constant and inescapable contact with cultural and interpersonal sources of anxiety. The self system functions solely for the purpose of avoiding anxiety and because it seeks such an important goal it eventually develops into a stable, self-perpetuating and independent aspect of the personality system. As a consequence, the self system is extremely resistant to change and can provide a potent barrier to social maturity and is often the stumbling block to favourable changes in a personality.

The contributions of psychoanalysts to self theory have been important not only for their theoretical contributions to the study of the problems of identity but for their attempts at an integrative theory of self. Jacobson (1965) has argued that a realistic self concept develops from images of self which become unified, organized and integrated through advancing psychosexual and ego development, maturational and other developmental processes making for increased capacity for perception and self-perception. If the developmental needs of the child are not met appropriately at each stage of development the regulation of self-esteem becomes faulty and the person becomes fixated at an infantile level knowing only extremes of perfection or destruction. To ward off the trauma of destruction an unreal, flawless self-image is created to compensate for the unacceptable face of the self in reality. The uses of the false self interferes with the accurate creation of a sense of self-esteem and in spite of all outward signs to the contrary the individual's personality is seriously flawed and the person feels worthless underneath (Reich, 1960; De Saussure, 1971). Recent psychoanalytical studies such as these are more concerned with problems of self-concept and self-esteem than with the sexual and oedipal problems of classical psychoanalysis, and this is especially true in the important writings of Kohut (1971, 1977), Wolf (1976) and Wolf, Gedo and Terman (1972). Wolf and his colleagues have discussed recent advances in outlining basic concepts in self psychology and shown the importance of adolescence as a period in which the adolescent process may be seen as a transformation of self. Kohut has stressed the importance of realistic self-esteem based on socially useful, adaptive and joyful, healthy 'narcissism' shown throughout life by the pride we take in our endeavours and a love and acceptance of ourselves regardless of our short-comings. Kohut in revising a traditional theory of narcissism has linked it with the psychology of self and in a major deviation from Freud elevates self-love to a status equal to that of love of others and an important element in human creativity, wisdom, and empathy for our fellow man and woman.

Integrative Theories

Other theorists than psychoanalysts have attempted integrative theories of self. Snygg and Combs (1949) saw personality wholly in terms of the individual's personal conception of the current situation – his phenomenal field – and developed concepts of the Not-Self or Environment and the Phenomenal Self. Their view that self-consistency was essential to avoid personal stress led them to believe that there was only one motive for behaviour, the need for personal adequacy, and they felt that they had produced a global and all-inclusive psychological theory which solved all problems of motivation and learning. Their sources included 'Self-Consistency: a theory of personality' (Lecky 1945) but they and Lecky failed to explain adequately the many variables making up the personality and their theory was in itself incomplete and provided no scientific advance in the explanation of individual growth. Similarly, Bertocci (1945), in an ambitious attempt to relate the concepts of self and ego to personality structure had failed to find the source of human behaviour by merely discussing concepts and as Lowe (1961) comments the discussion by Bertocci on the nature of mind seemed to add little that seemed relevant for either experimental or applied psychology.

However, Bertocci himself had been at pains to show that the self did not explain the existence of any one system or any specific development within personality, that it had no specific experimental value, but he went on to say that if we experiment in order to improve our understanding and interpretation of human experience, then self might be found useful as an integrative concept, even though it might need modification or expansion in the light of empirical data. Bertocci, to this writer at least, seems to be arguing that although the self-concept had perhaps fallen prey to psychoanalysts and sociologists it was still a necessary concept in psychology. There were major psychologists willing to support such a claim. The calibre of Allport as a psychologist of personality forced more behavioural psychologists to recognize the self as a field of study. D.O. Hebb argued persuasively that psychologists should tackle the self-concept while Hilgard concluded than an understanding of related psychological fields demanded a concept of self in psychology (Diggory, 1965). Ruth Wylie in her classic 1961 study of self-concept stressed the theoretical importance of self-concept, though she and others rightly pointed out the difficulties involved in studying the construct and related areas of study (Crowne and Stephens, 1961; Wylie, 1961). The work of Gardner Murphy made theories of self central to the study of personality and, like Mead before him, he saw the self defined via social processes, but aided by the perception of the child. This perceptual process might be hastened by the arrival of language, e.g. the pronouns 'mine', 'you' and 'I' might be seen as conceptual valuations of the self. Social contact, play and similar experiences add to the growing self-concept and the process of identification hastens it forward, as do projection and introjection until by the age of three the self picture is fairly well integrated. As the picture becomes more established, the child becomes less a perceptual object and more a conceptual trait system. Experiences in school finalize the self picture: proneness to a particular behaviour is recognized as one's own and in due course becomes a prominent feature of the self (Murphy, 1947).

Humanistic Psychology

A major boost to the study of self-concept came with the emergence of humanistic psychology in the 1950's. Humanistic psychology was primarily concerned with the idea of personal growth and the view that man is positive in his nature, is basically socialized, progressive, rational and realistic. Its theorists saw behaviourism as too mechanical a doctrine because it failed to satisfactorily account for the specifically human characteristics in people and they regarded orthodox psychoanalysis as basically pessimistic in its view of human nature for Freud saw men and women always on the defensive. Main contributors to humanistic psychology were Perls, Maslow and Carl Rogers. Perls believed that people could deepen their own self-awareness if they had the courage and strength to be open to experience and the full range of feelings from despair to ecstasy. This greater understanding of experience would allow men and women to be emotionally self-sufficient, to use their own resources, run their own lives, and achieve a sense of personal authenticity. Maslow pushed the idea of self-actualization as a normal and universal process of growth (Bayne, 1977). The self is seen as essentially sound but covered by 'trappings of roles and relationships which have produced a whole set of false self-images' (Rowan, 1975). If someone can tap his basic self and allow it to integrate his activities it will allow him to reach goals based on his own standards and to achieve the self-confidence and self-respect which will allow him to become a fully-functioning person. It is possible to relate this theory to that of Loevinger on ego-development and see the work of Maslow as very far-reaching indeed, calling for a complete shake-up in existing society and values, but its critics would regard Maslow as a naive idealist and see the number of completely self-actualizing individuals as few indeed, and if one were very cynical, as middle class American professors. The writings and theories of Carl Rogers are likely to be more enduring and more amenable to empirical research, and in his many writings he has greatly increased the respectability of the self as a psychological concept. His emphasis on client-centred therapy and the analysis of person to person relationships has not only made his work widely known to practitioners in teaching and the helping professions, but placed self-concept as a central construct in personality theory and counselling theory for Rogers is most interested in the clients, and increasingly in the pupil's self-conception, strongly believing in the self-realizing potential of a person (Rogers, 1951, 1962). Rogers believes that if a person can accept himself he will grow to greater emotional maturity and have no need of defence mechanisms as he revises his view of himself and others for Rogers proposes that all persons develop a self-concept of themselves which serves to guide and maintain their adjustment to the external world. This image develops out of social experience and if through social interaction the individual makes harsh, rejecting images of himself he produces doubts of his worthiness and competence and causes stress to himself and others. Rogers has argued in his many writings that a permissive atmosphere where parents are willing to accept differences and are able to trust their children will enable the individual to know and accept himself. The Rogerian theory of self-concept might well be described as it is by Moustakas (1956) as 'exploration in personal growth'.

Vernon (1964) has pointed out the particular relevance of Rogerian theory to educational problems but it is probably Hilgard (1949), in attempting to integrate the concept of self with Freud's writings on the mechanisms of psychological defence, who not only most emphasizes the relevance of self-concept study for the teacher, especially in stressing how self-conception may motivate the individual to goal achievement, but who probably most restored self-concept as a respectable study area in academic psychology when he made it the subject of his presidential address to the prestigious American Psychological Association. Hilgard saw the self as a product of interpersonal influences and probably having only a full meaning when expressed in social interactions. Since Hilgard, studies of self-concept have spread into many areas of pure and applied psychology (Bayne, 1977; Cozby, 1973; Thomas, 1973; Shaw, 1974) with an increasing variety of terms and methodology.

Self and Educational Practice

The ever increasing attention given to the individual in education will inevitably stress differences between separate individuals' academic and social development. Learning performance is affected not only by intelligence but also by personality, and personality also relates to levels of maturation and anxiety. Empirical evidence on personality and learning points to a relationship between learning and personality type. Self theory is an important area of personality studies and experiences in school contribute to the development of self and the process of identification with parents now gives way to a self picture that is one's own. When a pupil is singled out for praise or blame, his self is given the role of good or bad entities for this is determined by one's good or bad behaviour. Proneness to a particular way of behaving is recognized as one's own and in time becomes a prominent feature of the self-concept. Improving low self-confidence is important for learning, and underlines again the importance of self theory for the teacher, for the self is an essential part of the learning process and so is of primary concern for all those interested in any way in the growth of children.

If the self is learned then awareness of it in the pupil can be consciously taught by the teacher. Jersild (1951) complained that the teaching of self-understanding was evaded in schools and proposed that the aim of education should be to help the growing person while he is in the process of adjusting to conditions within himself, to help him realize his capacities and abilities, control his emotions, appreciate his strengths and weaknesses, and set himself realistic goals. Probably the most important facts in a child's life are his relationships with others and his relationship to himself, and Jersild pleads that 'learning which pertains to anything so crucial should properly be part of the child's education and indeed should be regarded as the most important of the educational program'.

Adolescence

This programme of teaching pupils about their self development is perhaps most important in adolescence for many psychologists would argue that adult maturity cannot be achieved without some relatively serious self-conflict during the teenage years. Wall, especially, has made self-concept a key idea in his writings on adolescence, both in his synthesis work of a decade ago and in his more recent theoretical and interdisciplinary approach to adolescence (Wall, 1968, 1977). He suggests that the road to maturity lies through the sound construction of five selves – physical, sexual, vocational, social and philosophical. The achievement of adult status incorporating these five selves may be said to formulate the general goals of young people in modern Western or Westernized societies. The teaching and counselling staff of schools and colleges can create security or reassurance for the emergence of the five selves and provide information and guidance to the adolescent for making responsible choices in what Hemming (1966) has called the struggle for self-fulfilment in the developmental tasks of dealing with the heightened emotionality of adolescence, attaining personal identity, establishing good relationships with peers, developing sexual adjustments, attaining recognition by and acceptance from adults, and finding a set of values by which to live. Hemming suggests that to give up this struggle for self-fulfilment is a form of personal betrayal and has developed this theme in pointing out the relevance of self-value in the development of individual and community morality, 'for a well-founded sense of self-value with its concomitant self-confidence is the sine qua non of moral development' (Hemming, 1971). Without adequate feelings of self-value one has an inadequate sense of responsibility. It can be argued that this relationship between self-value, self-confidence and moral development needs much more attention in schools, especially as the competitive nature of much education may counteract the enhancement of such relationships. Self values are not only important for the community life of the individual but, in reverse, community values are relevant to the development of self-esteem and these community values operate throughout the school years and often the school is the institution through which those values are transmitted to the individual child. Certainly the school may be arguably even more important today in this connection at a time when the present day social order of complex large scale organizations gives little nourishment to self. Some writers such as Young (1972) would regard the need for self as a source of social and public order for only through understanding of our selves may we humanize technology.

Curriculum

These values of self would be more easily transmitted if self-education could be structured into the curriculum for there is rich opportunity for self-reference in many school subjects and a case to be made out for teaching psychology, especially developmental psychology, to adolescents, but schools could do much more in this respect. Richer (1968) concluded that pupils felt that teachers rejected the personalities of less able and average children, that pupils were not treated as persons or taught to seek responsibility and be self-critical. Richer comments that teachers primarily see schooling as a system of social control, basically custodial, and informal behaviour is seen as taking place in areas and activities defined by the staff. As a result many children are disobedient, apathetic, or neurotic and become skilled at developing a false self-system capable of protecting and defending the real self. If the strongest need of the individual is the satisfaction of a realistic self image then it would seem that schools are geared to defeat this aim, that students moving from schools to colleges are often characterized by feelings of low self-worth and inferiority and that ex-pupils emphasize the failure of their schools to respect their selves and treat them as personalities. Many pupils asked to participate in the planning of a curriculum or a syllabus would make demands for a greater emphasis on the developmental tasks of adolescence: in summary would want more opportunity for education of the self. Interestingly there are now perhaps signs that institutionalized education is beginning to pay greater attention to adolescent needs and that recent curriculum projects in areas as diverse as moral education, humanities and technology, are beginning to provide opportunities for the young adult to prove his competence and establish understanding. Similarly, pleas are made to increase self-understanding in courses of teacher education and in undergraduate courses in psychology (Bayne, 1973, 1974; Laidlaw, 1974; Wall, 1977).

Self and the Teacher

The need for greater attention to the self in education was implied by Havighurst, Robinson and Dorr (1946): 'it is clear that the schools, churches and youth serving agencies influence the ideals of youth as much or more through the presence and behaviour of teachers, clergy and youth leaders as through their verbal teaching'. Staines (1958) demonstrated that teacher behaviour can make specific changes in the pupil self-picture and Hogan and Green (1971) have described the organization of in-service teachers' workshops to make teachers aware that they are able to modify the self-concepts of children and they argued that continuing professional education for the teachers should include cognitive and affective activities that will help enhance the images that pupils have of themselves. Davidson and Lang (1960) showed how perceptions by children of their teachers' feelings towards them related to self-perception, achievement and school behaviour, while Perkins (1958) revealed that those teachers who attended courses in child study helped reduce discrepancies between a pupil's actual and ideal self-concepts. Many teachers, however, still need to realize their potential in aiding the growth of pupils' selves partly because they underestimate the importance of their own selves in educating the selves of others. Combs (1965) points out that teachers too are individuals who must have self-discipline and seek to be persons in their own right, while Menninger (1953) suggests that self-understanding for teachers must be a necessary prerequisite of teaching children to appreciate their own selves. Teachers, not only pupils, must recognize the need to improve their own behaviour, to maintain their mental health, to get satisfaction through self-sufficiency, to be emotionally mature and to learn to profit from personal mistakes and successes: in Comb's phrase 'each of us must seek to become the very best self he can be'.

Chapter 3

Development of Self-concept I

This chapter and Chapter 4 survey the literature on the development of self-concept in childhood and adolescence. A number of studies are looked at in an attempt to cover the following areas: determinants and development of self-concept; ideal self; stages and structure of self development; sex differences; body concept; minority group self-concept; self-concept of the handicapped.

Determinants of Self-concept

Positive self-concept is a necessary prerequisite for human happiness in any situation and any teacher accepting pastoral care and counselling as part of his role benefits from a knowledge of the determinants of self-concept. These determinants, in order of importance as influences on self development, are the home and the school. These two factors are probably of greater importance for the growth of self-concept than is the social class of which a person is a member. The number of investigations of relationship between self-concept and socio-economic status is increasing but the total picture is confused. Trowbridge (1972) has pointed out that some studies show that children of low socio-economic status actually reflect the negative image society has of them while by other criteria some studies indicate that the self-concept of low socio-economic status children may be even more positive than that of middle class children. It would be fallacious to assume that the lower the social class of the child the lower his self-esteem.

There is no disagreement that the parent-child relationship is a very important determinant of self-concept. Mistry (1960) showed that emotional security with parents is essential for the development of positive self-concept. Where the spirit of the child's home was one of warmth, mutual respect and consideration the child developed a realistic concept of himself. The unpublished findings of Carlson (1958) and Silver (1958) support this view, and Rosenberg (1963) indicates that when parents were indifferent towards their children, the children later showed low degrees of self-esteem. Washburn (1962) argues that parents who are too strict, insufficiently protective, or over-critical may interfere with the attainment by their children of a mature self-concept. The father's attitude, if over-critical and highly unprotective, reduces the adolescent's opinion of himself.

Such studies, in emphasizing the climate of the home as a determinant of self-concept, are supported by probably the best known study in this area, that of Coopersmith (1967) who concluded that the determinants of self-esteem are a combination of the following conditions: total, or nearly total, acceptance by parents of their children; clearly defined, enforced limits of permissible behaviour; respect and latitude for individual action within defined limits; high parental self-esteem. The presence of one alone of these conditions reveal general family relationships which show that parental limits and rules are likely to facilitate positive self-concepts and that parental performance within such limits is likely to be moderate, tolerant, and generally civilized with children viewing their parents with greater affection and respect. Zahran (1967) also notes the close relationship between self-evaluation and evaluation of the family relationship, while, in a major study, Rosenberg (1965) argued that adolescents who had closer relationships with their fathers were higher in self-esteem than those with more distant, impersonal relationships, and found that the amount of parental interest and concern is significantly related to self-concept. Wright and Tuska (1966) in an interesting study of femininity quoted recollections of an emotionally satisfying mother and a successful father as characteristics of the 'feminine' woman and recollections of an emotionally satisfying father but a frustrating, unsympathetic mother characterized the 'masculine' woman. Wooster and Harris (1972) found some support for their hypothesis that the mobile life of service parents deprives their children of opportunities to develop their self-concept to the level of their geographically stable peers.

Most of the studies relating child self-concept to family life show the importance of parents as models in the socialization of the child. They indicate that lack of parental attention, absence of affection, lack of firm rules, severe punishment, and family tension have an adverse affect on self-concept development and depress levels of self-esteem. Research to date generally pays more attention to the role of the mother than to that of the father and further studies are needed of the paternal self-concept and its effect on the self-concept of the child.

The school and peer influences also affect the development of the self-concept. The importance of the school as an organization is the subject of a separate chapter in this book but it is essential to state here that the school is second only to the home in determining an individual's views on self-acceptance and self-rejection. Once a child becomes convinced that school is not a place for him, that it is a place of anxiety and threats to his identity, it becomes extremely difficult to rescue both teachers and pupils from a complex situation. It may well be, as in Morse (1964), that for some children the image of school grows more negative with time and communicates to them a learned and constantly reinforced sense of inadequacy. Peer groups and interpersonal relationships play their part in determining self-concept. Carlson (1958) found a positive correlation between self-concept and peer status. Silver (1958) concluded that the level of self-concept ratings of children was a measure of interpersonal attraction. Griffitt ((1969) showed that attraction of undergraduates to each other was significantly affected by the similarity of their self-concepts, while a paper by Kipnis (1961) also proposes positive evaluation of friends as a major factor in later self-evaluation. Archer (1974) found that the relative power of persons within their groups was a fairly strong predictor of the direction of self-concept changes: persons high in power changed towards a more positive self-concept and those low in power changed towards a more negative self-concept. Powerful group members received dividends that strengthened their positive view of self based on the realization that powerful group members have a disproportionate share of the attention of other group members.

Before leaving this section one should note the importance of temporary changes of mood on self-concept and levels of self-esteem. Wessman and Ricks (1966) demonstrated how self-concept varied considerably across the two emotional states of elation and depression, while personal ideals remained relatively constant. In depression, self-concepts tended to become more derogatory, indicating isolation from others and preoccupation with self. The self failed to meet ideals about important personal and academic goals and discrepancy between perceived self and ideal self was more acutely experienced in periods of depression. Elation was generally accompanied by a substantial increase in importance of family relationships in developing a positive sense of worth. The happy individuals in their study 'were able to make positive identifications with respected and approachable role models, which favoured the establishment and development of a worthwhile sense of self. Begun in the family, this continuing process was furthered as they moved into the world.'

Growth of Self-concept

The child learns about self from his parents, his successes and failures in human relationships, and from his social experiences. He builds up his frame of reference, learns to distinguish 'self' from 'other' and has a fairly well integrated self-concept by his third year of life. Early on children develop a social 'I' by observing the effect of their actions on others. As long ago as 1902 in 'Human Nature and the Social Order' C.H. Cooley gave an illustration of this from the autobiography of Charles Darwin: 'I once gathered much valuable fruit from my father's trees and hid it in the shrubbery, and then ran in breathless haste to spread the news that I had discovered a hoard of stolen fruit'. Cooley also quotes children at sixteen months with their repertoires of small performances carried out as part of self-assertive action for effect. Later there is a suppression by the child of more naive behaviour and the development of self-awareness becomes more subtle. Affection, indifference, or contempt may be simulated to hide the real wish to affect the self-image. It is important for young children that they see themselves as wanted and loved and, as Ira Gordon has written, 'for very young children, negative self-image may be as damaging as physical illness or actual physical handicap' (Gordon, 1969).

Language of young children may reveal the growth of self-awareness and Goodenough (1938) took the use of the first personal pronoun as evidence that at least a primitive step in development of self-concept had been reached. Bain (1936) interestingly recorded the speech of his own child who attempted to say her own name at fifteen months. Six months later 'Dadda bumps me' was recorded, and by twenty-seven months most of the 'self' and 'other' words seemed to be learned and used correctly most of the time. From one year on the 'self' becomes explosive, aggressive and strongly emotional. Becoming adult consists largely of disciplining the 'self' of childhood and learning to express it in socially acceptable ways which allow one to become a socialized person. The struggle for self-fulfilment beginning so early in life finds its greatest intensity in adolescence with the restructuring of emotional life that occurs in the teenage years.

Hemming (1974) has brought out the importance of self-concept in the dynamics of adolescent growth, where 'the perception of self determines the quality and extent of interaction with the external world and modifies personal development as a whole, including emotional and moral aspects'. Adolescents with strong self confidence have this reinforced and those who feel failures tend to live up to their own expectations. The teenager has to learn to live his own life rather than in terms of the expectations of others but the inner and outer world of the adolescent is in a state of flux which makes self development more difficult. The adolescent is conscious of self and the cherished image of what he wants to be accounts for his characteristic vulnerability to slight and shame. Self-esteem, writes Galdston (1967) is *the* issue of adolescence. The achievement of self-esteem constitutes the major developmental endeavour and is clearly evident in studies as varied as Emmett (1959), Hemming (1960), Veness (1962), Crow (1962), Coopersmith (1967), Zahran (1967), Offer (1969), Musgrove (1969) and Thompson (1974).

Rosenberg (1965) is a major cross-sectional study of 5,000 adolescents in the United States and indicates the characteristics of teenagers with low and high self-esteem. Low self-esteem individuals showed depression, anxiety and low average achievement. They felt they would never attain the success they desired or enter a preferred job because they saw themselves as lacking the assets essential for success in their chosen fields. The high self-esteem adolescents saw themselves as possessing: ability for self-expression; self-confidence; perseverance; leadership potential; talent; intelligence and skill; ability to make a good impression; social skills; practical knowledge; self-assurance. The contrast between the two groups is further emphasized by the low-esteem teenagers' feelings of social isolation. They believed that other people neither really understood nor respected them and were not to be trusted. Other people reacted to them in ways which only reinforced their own low expectations and lack of self-esteem.

Adolescent concern with identity which is a notable feature of the last study is the main theme of a British study of adolescent relationships with particular reference to Erikson's notions of identity crisis and identity diffusion (Coleman, 1974). This study of 347 boys and 392 girls in age-groups 11, 13, 15 and 17, reveals that the proportions of each age-group feeling negative about themselves is strikingly similar – 30 to 43 per cent, with almost identical development for both sexes. At no one stage are there signs of a greater disturbance or crisis in self-image than at any other and older adolescents appear the same as younger groups. A considerable minority of adolescents manifest issues of personal identity throughout the age-range while conflicts over future identity increase with age.

Stability of Self-concept

Little is known about stability and change in self-concept, though Harris (1971) did show scholastic self-concept to be a relatively stable dimension of personality for both early and middle adolescence. Engel (1959) and Carlson (1965) also suggest that self-concept and self-esteem are fairly stable aspects of development. Some studies such as Katz and Zigler (1967) and Bohan (1973) indicate a lower self-concept score for adolescents than for younger children, but these findings are contradicted by Piers and Harris (1964) and in the aforementioned study by Engel which found an increase in positive self-concept as children grow up. In general, aside from psychiatric case studies, there is little evidence on change of self-image from childhood to adolescence, and work as well known as the Engel study can be faulted on methodological grounds. The developmental period encompassed by the research was only a two-year span and conceptualization of self-concept was seemingly limited to a dimension of self-esteem. Some of the observed stability in the study may represent the responses of subjects in terms of the fairly obvious social desirability in the testing instrument.

One may emphasize the need for more work on the stability of self-concept and note the need to look for possible disturbance in the self-image at adolescence. Often, as Bledsoe and Wiggins (1973) noted, parents see their adolescent offspring in more favourable terms than do the adolescents in their own self-perceptions and the difficulties faced by adolescents may not always be clear to parents. It is not simply in how favourable a light an individual sees himself but how much he has staked himself on a particular quality. Low self-esteem on a quality highly valued is likely to be experienced as disturbing, even more so if it occurs at puberty with its attendant stresses. Simmons *et al.* (1973) have suggested that perhaps puberty heightens vulnerability to environmental stresses which threaten the self-concept and they found some evidence of self-image becoming more stable in later adolescence. We are unable to say with any certainty whether the level or type of self-concept disturbance which develops in adolescents persists in adult life, but some theorists would argue that later adult emotional problems might be explicable in terms of unsolved identity crises during adolescence. There are certainly studies like that of Brownfain (1952) which support the theoretical prediction that people with stable self-concepts are better adjusted than those with unstable self-concepts and will exhibit higher levels of self-esteem, fewer feelings of inferiority or neurosis, fewer instances of defensive behaviour, and greater social acceptance and social participation.

Ideal Self

The ideal self is the perception held by a person of what he or she would like to be physically and psychologically. It serves as an internalized standard made up of hopes and aspirations based on what the boy and girl or adolescent knows members of his or her group or culture value highly. The self-esteem of an individual will reflect whether his self-concept matches his ideal self, the greater the disparity between actual (or real) self and ideal self the greater will be the lack of self-esteem. Certain definite values will be reflected in the ideal self and, for example, in studies in Jamaica reported in Phillips (1973), it is not surprising to find an emphasis in the ideal self on material success. Jamaican society values people who are materially successful and the ideal towards which adolescents strive naturally incorporates this value. The ideal self of these Jamaican youngsters was one of a socially well-adjusted individual with good manners and behaviour, able to relate well with his peers, and particularly with the opposite sex. There were early glimpses too of the desire for love and marriage.

In many respects the Jamaican adolescents exhibit similar self values to those British youngsters studied by Eppel and Eppel (1966), except that in the latter study only one in eight subjects were predominantly materialistic. This lack of materialism is reflected in a replication of the Eppel study by Simmons (1980). It may reflect cultural differences, but it is surprising that the latter figure is so small given the images of 'success' purveyed by the popular press and the pressures of commercial advertising. It should also be noted that the U.K. study looked at working class adolescents whilst the Jamaican studies were of adolescents of higher socio-economic status, so the comparison is complicated by a host of cultural and class expectations. Both studies contain a range of idealized values through physical appearance, social acceptance, health and recreational concerns, intellectual values, aesthetic ideals, and moral values, apart from the economic concerns mentioned above.

The Eppel's technique was analysis of essays on the theme 'The Person I Would Most Like to Be Like'. The children took as models individuals varying from people whom they knew personally to well known public figures. Sometimes the picture presented is of a single character, sometimes a combination of two or more people. Occasionally the model of ideal self is not related to any real person but is a projection of the writer's fantasy ideal. Fathers, mothers, sisters, uncles, friends, provide models, and the extracts from the essays make fascinating reading. Similar extracts on the ideal self may be found in Strang (1957) where she gives an account of essays set for an adolescent group and supplemented her material with information from autobiographies. She also found adolescents much concerned with inner resources and with moral and spiritual values. Similar projective methods are illustrated in Thomas (1974) and in the work of Stern (1961) and Veness (1962). The first study of final year junior school children indicated physical, intellectual, and moral ideals, together with concerns about material possessions, marriage and parenthood. Stern asked grammar school boys to write brief forecasts of their personal and vocational futures. Nearly a decade later he followed up their careers and found that they had predicted very accurately. Their forecasts covered a range of careers, including accountancy, engineering, teaching, the R.A.F. and even fire fighting abroad! The pupils also predicted correctly personal details such as marital status, size of family and recreations. Veness, in a study of the retrospective autobiographies of school-leavers who were asked to imagine themselves at the end of their lives, found self-images focussing on academic or vocational ability, appearance, health and physique, and aspects of character. Olasehinde (1972) has examined the development of the ideal self in Nigerian children and gives useful references to studies of the ideal self in children of other non-European cultures.

The classic accounts of ideal self are still those of Havighurst *et al.* (1946) and Havighurst and MacDonald (1955), dealing with American and Australian children and young people respectively. Both studies find the same developmental trend, beginning with identification in early childhood with a parental figure and ending in late adolescence with the ideal self symbolized by an attractive adult or an imaginary person who is a composite of desirable qualities. Intermediate is a stage of romanticism, when the ideal self is an unreal, glamorous figure or a character in juvenile fiction with superhuman qualities. Some children seem to miss this intermediate stage, others experience it more quickly, others prolong it into late adolescence; and it is unclear if all children reach the composite stage. It is possible that many never achieve the ability to conceive of an ideal self who is composite or imaginary. The writers suggest that lower social class children tend to use a glamorous person as ideal self and fewer of them describe a composite figure than do children of a higher social class. However, concepts of ideal self may shift with social changes and invalidate such findings. It could also be argued that changes in self and ideal self conguency may reveal growth and development and reflect influences of school experience on a pupil. Havighurst makes no mention of sex differences or teacher influence, but Perkins (1958b) found the self and ideal self congruencies of girls to be significantly greater than those of the boys, while the children whose teachers had attended child study courses had greater congruencies than other children. Jervis (1959) found slight but significantly larger discrepancies between actual self and ideal self among college women than among college men. These differences are possibly accounted for in terms of the earlier physical maturity of women and the feminine mores of many school systems. It is important to stress how little is known about how girls and women see themselves, what their expectations and aspirations are and how they feel about personal relationships and questions of sex, marriage and parenthood. In a scholarly and valuable review of research Fransella and Frost (1977) suggest that women are faced on the one hand by a strong process of role identification mediated by rosy promises from a fantasy ideal and on the other hand, particularly as regards parenthood, by a distinctly grim and unfulfilling reality.

The adolescent uses his ideal self as part of the determining of his own personality. An unrealistic ideal may lead to the traumatic frustration of distraught idealism. In this way the ideal self may become an obstacle to the improvement of actual self. Another blocking effect of the ideal self on personality improvement is when the boy or girl may idealize a person not approved or admired by his social group or the dominant culture and its value system. In attempting to model his or her behaviour after that of his ideal, the adolescent may develop characteristics that will make him a social misfit and a candidate for maladjustment or delinquency.

Stages

Very few studies exist which attempt to identify stages in self-concept growth and even fewer attempts to identify such stages in terms of the developmental theory of Piaget. An important Piagetian informed approach is that contained in an unpublished Harvard Ph.D. thesis by Broughton (1975). My summary follows the longer exposition and discussion contained in Loevinger (1976). Broughton is presently seeking empirical confirmation of sequentiality of levels by means of longitudinal study.

Broughton proposed seven stages or levels of self-concept growth described as follows. In stage O, that of the pre-school child, thoughts are not distinguished from their actions: self is regarded as 'inside', reality as 'outside'. In stage 1, ages five and six, the self is the physical body, and bodily movement is regarded as changing the self. The child's view of reality is naive, and the author explicitly points out that at this level the relation of mind or brain to body is that of authority and he evokes (presumably following his subjects) a metaphor of a big person and a little person. Stage 2, from ages seven to twelve, sees the self as an individual person, including both mind and body. The self includes the child's reactions to and his ideas about things. Individuality resides in the uniqueness of these reactions and ideas. Knowledge is personal, and the distinction between facts and opinions is blurred. Stage 3, ages eleven to seventeen, sees the appearance of reflective self awareness. The self is not assumed to be automatically aware of itself as at earlier levels, and the mind is differentiated into conscious and unconscious. The self is what the nature of the adolescent normally is: conscious and controlled, contrasting with abnormal and unconscious. At stage 4, in late adolescence, the self becomes identified as experience and behaviour, and the person is a cybernetic system guided to fulfilment of its material wants. At level 5, the self as observer is distinguished from the inner self as impulse or desire. At the highest level of stage 6, mind and body are both experiences of an integrated self. What is true is a judgement, a construction of what may be universally experienced under properly controlled conditions.

Washburn (1961) has postulated a theory of self-conceptualization based on statistical treatment of data illustrating the theories of Erikson, Freud, Fromm, Horney and Sarbin. Six levels of self-conceptualization emerge which in order of increasing maturity are as follows: The Somatic – Primitive Self, concerned with the immediate qualification of needs; the Submissive – Dependent Self, involving avoidance of disapproval by submitting to others; Detached – Independent Self, fearing emotional involvement with others; Outer – Controlling Self, manipulating the environment to obtain approval as symbolized by social status; Inner – Controlled Self, involving the internalization of social norms which provide attitudes functioning to control behaviour; Integrating – Actualizing Self, involving acceptance of oneself and others and orientation towards self-fulfilment.

Structure

Models of structure of self-concept are presented in a number of writings, most notably in Jersild (1952). Jersild's well-known work indicated the material, spiritual and social selves as dimensions of self structure; his categories of self include physical characteristics, health, material possessions, personal relationships, school, intellectual status, social attitudes and other traits. The analysis of data revealed that responses made by his 3,000 children could be set out as an ascending order of psychological maturity beginning with physical self and ending with religious ideas and independence and self help. The general direction of Jersild's trends in self development are reflected in a number of studies. Thomson (1971) invited children in a rural primary school and eleven – fourteen year old pupils in a London secondary school to write anonymous essays on their self-images. The essays were then analysed using the categories described by Jersild and the categories tabulated against children's ages. The tabulation showed a movement from emphasis on physical appearance which occurs in the 7 – 8 age-group, to sports, games and hobbies of the nine-year-olds. The eleven – thirteen year-olds are concerned a little more about personality traits and the fourteen-year-old adolescents emphasize home, family and social relationships. Health and material ownership are mentioned very little at all ages, as is intellectual status. Topics of religion and independence are not mentioned until the fourteen-year-old age-group and this would confirm Jersild's procedure of setting them for later maturity. In another unpublished study of children's self-reports, Emmett (1959) found the main categories of self distinguished by his eleven – fifteen-year-olds to be personality, life goals, social attitudes, physical aspects, school, home and family, and material possessions. The important aspect of this research is the author's conclusion that the hypothesis that different age-groups emphasize or anchor on different aspects or items within the self does not appear to be supported, and that the noticeable feature is the diversity in patterns of self-concept as it is seen varying from child to child. Thomas (1971) found his seventy-six ten and eleven-year-olds emphasized physical, moral, social and academic aspects of their self development. Livesley and Bromley (1973) with self-report data from 320 British children found that categories of self showing decreasing frequency with age were those relating to objective information about themselves, e.g. appearance, information and identity, possessions, family and friends. Categories which increased as children grew up were those concerned with personal attributes, interests, beliefs and values, relationships with and attitudes to others. The information on the self was now better organized and more clearly expressed showing the adolescent demonstrating his or her need to 'establish himself as an individual with independence, balance, and a unified, consistent personality' (Burns, 1977). Strang (1957) argued for a four constituent structure of self: the basic self, the person he or she thinks he is; the transitory self at the present time; the social self as others see him or her; and the ideal self he or she hopes to be. Like Jersild, Strang regarded the self as a developmental phenomenon and saw spiritual values as the high point in self-concept growth.

Sex Differences in Self-concept

The writing on sex differences in self-concept would, on balance, indicate such differences, though Jervis (1959) found that the self descriptions of his sex groups were nearly identical, Matteson (1956) found no significant differences in self-estimates of college progress, and, Piers and Harris (1964) found no consistent self-concept differences between the sexes in school children in grades 3, 6 and 10.

Amatora (1945) found differences in self-ratings of elementary school boys and girls. Boys tended to underrate themselves as compared to their ratings by girls and teachers. Girls tended to overrate themselves on intelligence, sociability, neatness and quietness. Kohn and Fiedler (1961) found high school and college girls rated themselves higher on self-esteem scores than did boys, and the total sex difference was significant. Kosa, Rachiele and Schommer (1962) quote significant differences in college students, girls rating themselves academically less able than the boys. It is apparent, also, that markedly different sub-cultures may also lead to marked differences in the rating of different sexes, as Phillips (1964) found in a teacher training situation, while sex role identity is an important aspect of self-conceptualization with positive feelings as to one's maleness or femaleness essential for development, and where sex role identity may impede or help academic achievement. Ponzo and Wrag Strowig (1973) showed that feminine orientated girls tended to become more traditionally feminine, while boys who were unsure of their masculinity strove to demonstrate their masculinity in ways that impeded achievement. It was felt that schools tended to promulgate the traditional feminine role rather than allowing girls freedom to develop according to their own abilities and self-knowledge. Bohan (1973) indicated that adolescent girls showed a marked drop in self-concept compared to male peers and younger girls. As the adolescent girl comes to recognize that the role she is expected to assume as a female is relatively inferior in prestige to the male role, the assumption of her sexual role results in a corresponding decrease in her own evaluation of herself. The adolescent girl accepts and internalizes the cultural evaluation of her role as inferior and so values herself lowly. In contrast the male recognizes his role in society as a relatively highly valued one. It should be mentioned, however, that sexual discrimination against girls does not necessarily lead to a lowering of the female self-concept. Weinreich (1978) in a study of indigenous adolescents and of West Indian and Asian adolescents in Bristol found no support for the argument that sex discrimination results in self-devaluation in girls. Bristol girls did not devalue themselves compared with boys, and this was found in all three ethnic groups. Yet it remains to be said that the problem of sex-role identity and sexual differences in self-conceptualization lie at the heart of the continuing basic problem of the severe underachievement of girls and women in advanced societies.

Differences in level of self-concept reached by subjects have also been examined. Washburn (1961) reporting an investigation with high school students, suggests that high activity levels are more likely to depress mature self levels in boys than in girls. Emotionality also seems related in boys to a lower self-concept level but no such relationship was found in girls. Carlson (1965), in a longitudinal study of high school students through early adolescence, found no sex differences in either level or stability of self-esteem; social orientation in the pre-adolescent was associated with declining self-esteem over a six-year-period for girls, but no trends were evident in the boys' data. Carlson suggests that self-esteem is a relatively stable dimension of self and is independent of sex role, though sex differences must be considered in thinking about the development and dynamics of the self-concept. Herman (1971), found significant sex differences in tenth grade students, with girls more concerned with weight, appearance, personal relationships, and boys more concerned with school progress. Veness (1962) also found boys more concerned than girls with school progress, and this may cause us no surprise if girls are able enough to perceive the inequality of opportunity for the sexes within the educational system, an inequality discussed in a much wider context by Eileen Byrne (1978) in 'Women and Education'.

Studies of the structure of self-concept also reveal sex differences. Amatora (1957) found girls above boys on ratings for punctuality, courtesy, honesty, patience, humour, and some other scales, and consistently higher on religion and neatness at all levels. It is unclear, however, if these are real differences in conceptualization or arise either from girls' earlier maturity or a tendency on the girls' part to overrate themselves. Kagan, Hosken and Watson (1961) using projective techniques and interviews with ninety-eight children aged six to eight, found that, in comparison to girls, boys labelled themselves stronger, larger, more dangerous, darker, more angular. Slee (1968) regards sex differences in self-concept as important for curriculum planning, for his girls revealed a feminine image factor in regard to school subjects, showing a liking for housecraft, art and music. It could be argued that curriculum choices themselves help to produce rather than reflect a feminine self-concept, and in any case the feminine image is not necessarily going to be uniform for some girls may see themselves as mothers whereas others see themselves as career women. Zahran (1967), in a study of 170 adolescents, found that girls scored higher on, among others, sociability, dependence, sensitivity, and tolerance. Boys were more confident, more self-acceptant, more dominant and realistic in their self-images. He also points out that sex differences in self-concept are sometimes so large that one cannot defend mixing the sexes as subjects in empirical studies of self-concept.

Chapter 4

Development of Self-concept II

Body Concept and Physical Development

As children grow and develop they find out what their bodies can do, discovering their body parts and learning different ways of using their physical development. Body movement allows for growth in other self-concept dimensions as well, so that by adolescence the changing form of the body becomes an important factor as an object of self-feelings and as a source of variation in self-concept. Adolescents observe the physiques of others and measure them against their own real and ideal bodies. Satisfaction with the physical self is important in the building of self-esteem which is a major developmental task in adolescence, and the greater the deviation of physical characteristics from preferred dimensions the greater the negative feelings towards those body parts and the self. The complexity of body awareness in self-concept in adolescents is further complicated by the developing of sexual roles and the consciousness of sexuality during the teenage years. This is well illustrated in Crow (1962) where the girl diarist writes: 'I am moody lately. I think I need a boyfriend. But who would like me? Short, fat and ugly'.

The relationship between body image and self is remarked on by personality theorists (Fisher and Cleveland, 1958; Fisher, 1970) and is marked in the writings and ratings of children and adolescents. In over 2,000 comments made by ten and eleven-year-olds in composition data on self, 27 per cent were concerned with aspects of physical appearance (Thomas, 1974). An important paper by Staffieri (1972) shows social stereotypes of body image developing in boys. The mesomorph body type was seen to represent an ideal male physique. The favourable stereotype of the mesomorph is evident at six years of age;

the preference to look like the mesomorph appears at age seven and is clearly established at eight years, when boys of eight and older report self-perceptions quite accurately and clearly prefer to look like the mesomorph image. The point at which accurate perceptions of body image become apparent (probably eight to nine years of age) may also be the start of dissatisfaction with one's body, and the degree of dissatisfaction may well be proportional to the extent that one's body differs from the mesomorph image. Similarly, Elder (1968) stresses cultural influences on body images with ideals of the human figure transmitted by parents, peers and the mass media. Through this process they acquire emotional significance and influence body and self-image when used as standards for evaluation of physical characteristics. Secord and Jourard (1953) found satisfaction with body parts strongly correlated with positive self-concepts, dissatisfaction with anxiety and insecurity. Cultural influence was emphasized by the same authors (Jourard and Secord, 1954) when satisfaction of males with height, weight and muscular strength varied by extent or size in accord with American cultural values. The culture infuences body image via the status hierarchy. The aforementioned paper by Elder pointed out that for the adolescent boy a physique that enables athletic success, attracts girls, and lacks femininity confers social status on him. Stoltz and Stoltz (1944) found boys emphasized athleticism, attraction to girls and lack of girlish characteristics, while girls were given status if attractive in face and figure, well-groomed and sophisticated. Status helps facilitate social skills and self-confidence and influences the self-concept. Studies of self-concept in girls (Hall, 1963; Lahiry, 1960; Calden, 1959; Herman, 1971) and of adolescent problems (Hemming, 1960) all indicate that girls show considerable dissatisfaction with their physical self, and are anxious about their failure to reach an ideal. Jourard and Secord (1955) found college girls rated preferred size of hips, waist and weight significantly smaller than their actual size, while preferred bust size was larger than self-reported size. None of the women had the figure she considered desirable and this deviation from the cultural ideal may cause low self-esteem. Miller (1967) found that the ideal figure for the Jamaican girl was a big bust, small waist, broad hips and long legs. The Caucasian ideal was still operative in Jamaica and, as noted in a review of other studies of the physical self in Jamaica, for many Jamaican adolescents there must be self-rejection of body-image. (Phillips, 1973). Gunderson (1965) in an investigation of young navy youths, found that the greater the deviation between actual and ideal physical self, the greater the likelihood of negative self-images and devaluation in self-assessment. Height in particular had a pervasive effect on self-evaluation, with short underweight and short overweight men having the most negative self-pictures. Obviously the environment of these particular subjects emphasized physique but, in that they illustrate the influence of sub-culture on self-concept, the findings may be generalized to other groups.

Maturation

Rate of physical maturation influences self-concept and the rate of growing up obviously involves reaching adult size and years and providing this developmental goal is reached adolescents do not wish to depart from the societal ideal for each sex. Early or slow development though is cause for concern in the individual (Lahiry, 1960). In the study by Frazier and Lisonbee (1950) girls often worried about early development and boys about slow development, while in Miller (1968) those girls who had not experienced puberty felt threatened by the lack of an adult body or feared the consequences of having one and their body-image remained a source of anxiety until they had achieved adult proportions. Whether physical deviations lead to a low sense of personal worth will depend partly on parental attitude, but it is clear that early and late maturers experience differences in self-concept and, in some studies, have differences in personality structure easily perceived by outsiders, e.g. in Jones and Bayley (1950) the peers of late-developing boys saw them as more attention seeking, restless and bossy, but less grown up and less good looking than early maturing boys. Jones and Mussen (1958) found early maturing girls had significantly more favourable self-concepts than late maturers, while late maturing adolescents of both sexes were characterized by less adequate self-concepts, slightly poorer parent-child relationships, and stronger dependency needs. Though the evidence from Jamaica summarized in Phillips (1973) would support these findings, there are cultural differences to be found in comparative studies of adolescence. Mussen and Boutourline-Young (1964) show that the effects of early and late maturing on self-conceptions and self-evaluations are much more marked among American boys than among Italian boys. American and Italian-American late maturers are more likely to suffer from feelings of inferiority, inadequacy, and rejection than are their more early developed companions. On the other hand, the relative rate of maturing does not appear noticeably to affect the personality structure of Italian boys in Italy, perhaps because physical size and strength and hence the characteristics of 'maturity' and 'independence' are not as highly prized in Italian culture as they would be in the United States. Rate of maturing is not the only factor contributing to the development of body concept as expressed in personality, and, in any person, individual experience will modify the effects of early or late maturing. One would suggest that children should be encouraged to accept their physical selves and potential, for, on the evidence of counselling (Brownfain, 1952; Taylor and Combs, 1952), the more self-acceptant the child the better adjusted he becomes. Low opinion of oneself devalues the self and this leads to defensive attitudes and distorted perception of self and others (Washburn, 1961), while in some psychiatric conditions in adolescence the body image itself may become distorted (Irwin, 1978). Many discipline problems in school may stem from loss of self-esteem through low evaluation of the physical self, and Tanner (1978) has written convincingly of the implications for educational practice and policy of differences in adolescent growth rates and their attendant emotional characteristics.

Physical Education

The educator most directly helped or hindered in his work by the physical aspects of self-concept as seen by his or her pupils is the teacher of physical education, for the child who sees his or her physical self in a positive way as strong and athletic, and possesses good body awareness, is likely to be well-motivated towards physical activity. Conversely, the child who sees himself as weak and underweight may never realize a potential for physical activities because of adverse attitudes to physical education arising from his negative self-concept. Though teachers need to be aware of these problems as argued in Thomas (1978), it is interesting that those pupils who have physical prowess are not necessarily higher in self-concept than are other people (Ibrahim and Morrison, 1976). This is understandable in view of the work of psychologists of sport who would argue that body-image is more complex than some self theorists and experimenters suggest and may have at least three dimensions – 'a sensory - spatial dimension, an existential dimension and a valuative dimension' where it is further possible that each dimension may well be subject to different cultural norms (Kane, 1978). Readers wishing to follow up the literature on self-concept and physical education are referred to Harris (1973), Kane (1972), Whiting (1973) and Glencross (1978).

Appearance

Before leaving the body image we must briefly consider the place of general appearance in self-concept development for obviously appearance influences those reactions of others, comparisons with others, and identification with models which are the origins of self-picture and self-esteem. Goffman (1956) in his classic study on the presentation of self in everyday life has pointed out that dress, gesture and appearance are very important constituents in giving information to other people and the individual, wanting to create impressions as favourable to himself as possible, may deal in a great deal of deception, consciously or in other ways. The handicapped individual may be limited by his incapacity from building up satisfactorily complete self-images either because of the attitudes he perceives in society or because of the nature of his disability, for example, the blind are denied what has been called the unique sociological function of the eye (Goffman, 1968, 1969). Argyle (1969) provides a general discussion of this area and Stone (1962) complains of the way in which G.H. Mead and other symbolic interactionists neglected appearance and its effect through the reflected image of others back on the self. In appearance, Stone sees selves as established and mobilized in a process starting with childhood in the adage of 'blue for a boy and pink for a girl'. Early representation of the self is formulated in play which is facilitated by costume. Adult participation in the many games of life is again always represented by appropriate dress which assists the players in identifying each other. Stone notes that in looking at self one should look 'at the cloth, on which, as Carlyle noted long ago, society may in fact be founded'. Empirical work on appearance in self-concept is slowly increasing and an interesting study by Musa and Roach (1973) sees boys more often than girls rating their own appearance as more desirable than their peers. Among the boys nearly 44 per cent were sufficiently satisfied with their appearance and desired no change, but, in contrast, only 12 per cent of girls showed no desire to change anything about their appearance. Appearance acts as a symbol of self and is only one of many status symbols for the young falling into the display area. What you wear, drive, or play, is what matters and the adolescent wields the magic of dress and mannerism as a part of his armoury for asserting self-consciousness (Galdston, 1967). Appearance is one of many symbols and Hurlock (1974) contains an interesting discussion of others: names and nicknames, speech, age, success and reputation. All such symbols are the cues by which a person is judged by others and influence one's concept of self.

Ethnic Differences

It is not racist to consider ethnic differences in patterns of self-concept but of practical political and educational importance for the understanding of the psychology of race relations and multicultural education. Such studies of ethnic self-image appear to show in recent work a shift which allows for a more positive view to be taken of the self-concept of minority groups. Much work in the past three decades has been pessimistic about the self-concepts of minority ethnic groups and has seen the children of such groups as expressing low self-esteem. One reason for this was the equation of membership of such groups with cultural disadvantage. It was argued that lower estimates of school ability and achievement, and lower scholastic and career aspirations for lower social class adolescents would suggest less positive self-perceptions. Long (1969) pointed out that lower self-esteem for the lower class child was to be found in such diverse cultures as those of India, Barbados and urban Canada where such findings seemed sensible since environmental conditions were obviously harsher for children of lower socio-economic status. Trent (1957) had argued that given the historical prejudice against the black child, it should be recognized that pressures, unfairness, and hostility from the general community would make it more difficult for him to evaluate himself and others in a healthy fashion. The length of time spent in a host community might also be reflected in levels of self-concept as Gecas (1973) showed in an exploration of the self-conceptions of poor, rural migrant and settled Mexican-Americans. The migrants had a more favourable view of themselves than did the settled Mexican-Americans with regard to general evaluation and specific references to moral worth, confidence, self-determination and altruism. In another study of Mexican-Americans, Hishiki (1969) has pointed out the limited range of experiences open to a minority population and stressed the role of the school in providing every opportunity for the minority group. The studies of Mexican-Americans remind us that studying ethnic differences in self-images is more than just a comparison of blacks and whites. Brody (1968) surveys the range of minority groups in the United States, and has chapters on negroes, Puerto-Ricans, Mexicans, Chinese, Japanese and Red Indian Americans. He describes the lack of self-respect in many minority group adolescents and stresses the importance of studying self-concept growth against the historical and cultural backgrounds of their respective groups including the family structure and family attitudes. Minority groups should not be regarded as all alike and cultural changes within a group may lead to problems, for in the transition from one way of life to another the process of self-definition may become a confusing one, as is shown for Chinese adolescents in the USA, while the breakdown of traditional Apache life, especially for the urbanized Apache, has led to negative identities and fantasy life in the self-concept of Apache adolescents. Similarly it would be a mistake to regard all ethnic minorities in Britain as exhibiting similar concepts; for example, Hill (1974, 1975) found more positive attitudes in terms of self-concept amongst West Indian adolescents than amongst the Asians, especially the Pakistanis, and Bagley, Bart and Wong (1978) found the self-concepts of different groups of West Indian ten-year-olds in London varied with the language ability, years of schooling, material circumstances, and social attitudes of the parents. Where the parents were culturally disadvantaged and passively accepted alienating forces in English society the children had poor self-images.

In the last named study the socializing role of society and home in depressing self-concept is a major issue and from all over the world it is possible to produce studies indicating the depressing effect of belonging to a minority or persecuted group. Negro children not yet aged five can sense that they are stigmatized and grow uneasy and Goodman (1964) has commented that in the experience of being disadvantaged lies 'the dynamics for rendering personality asunder'. De Vos (1968) shows that in spite of their full legal equality the pariah caste of Japanese known as Eta have children who, wherever systematic comparisons with other groups have been made, always appear inferior and perform poorly compared with the majority groups. This difference occurs even when the children are taught in integrated schools, for the Eta see themselves as inferior, an attitude having considerable influence on their educational and vocational behaviour. Bloom (1960) in a study of South African university students found that the non-whites communicated highly emotionally, sharply and without restraint, feelings of disability, insecurity and despair. Crain and Weisman (1972) argue that blacks born in northern ghettos in the United States experience violence, instability and unhappiness, and that self-esteem can only be maintained through increased self-assertion and competitiveness. In similar argument Bloom (1971) asserts that the Negro in the USA can never answer the question 'Who Am I?' truthfully and with satisfaction and pride, because the definition of the role of the Negro given to him by white society is one of low status and of rejection. The Negro often makes elaborate attempts to reduce the tensions of low self-esteem by idealizing white society. This idealized white self being unattainable he hates whites for rejecting him. Because he still identifies with the whites his hatred is deflected back on his own race. Psychiatrists, writes Bloom, often find a double hatred in black patients: hatred of a society that equates black with inferior, and, secondly, hatred of one's self, parents, and race, for making one black and therefore vulnerable. Negroes have social selves that suffer from carrying an image of low status, low aspirations, and conflicting perspectives. Bloom also notes the problems of identity on the African continent, quoting the traumatic effects on self-concept of being reclassified black in South Africa and giving the case study of the white child growing up in Zambia who found difficulty in perceiving her parents' wealthy black friends as 'African' because aged four and a half she had already associated poverty with being African and associated being white with wealth. Phillips (1973) reports that though, in the 1960's, the Negro acquired greater feeling of self-worth in West Indian society, the private attitudes of individuals remained largely negative: 'the whites still tend to feel superior towards him and the Negro still regrets and wishes to escape from his Negro heritage. At the same time he has an ambivalent attitude towards colour. At one moment he will be bitterly anti-white, and at another time he will be filled with fear and dislike of black people, maybe including himself'. Thus, though the slogan 'Black is beautiful' may initially enhance self-image, the view of the majority culture may still overwhelmingly affect the self-concept of the minority group child. King (1965) found that his Kingston adolescents took pride in their blackness but often idealized the physical characteristics of whites, like the fifteen year old boy who wrote 'I wish I could be born again and become a little cleaner', while Morland (1966) in a comparison of race awareness in northern and southern white and Negro pre-school children found not only were they aware of racial differences but that children of all groups would prefer to be white.

Increased Minority Self-esteem

Given the negative flavour of much of this quoted research, why is it possible for students of ethnic personality to now argue that there is recent evidence of growing self-esteem amongst minority groups? Firstly there is the theoretical case put forward by Baughman in his 1971 analysis of Black Americans. Historical changes in the late 1960s (e.g. 'Black is Beautiful') might invalidate earlier research. The fact that blacks *act* subservient is not evidence that they *feel* subservient and they may indeed protect their self-esteem by attributing their problems to external forces. There is some reason to believe that the prejudicial attitudes of whites reflect low self-esteem in the white population and that active discrimination is a compensatory mechanism, the goal of which is to strengthen the self-concept of the white. Lastly, Baughman argues, that as society becomes more racially mixed the black adolescent will protect his self-esteem by interpreting his inferior status as caused by the political and economic system and not caused by his ethnic origin. There is some empirical evidence to support this theory in Wendland (1967), McDonald and Gynther (1965), and in Powers (1971). Wendland argues that the black adolescent may react to the low status in which he is held by whites by interpreting this as an expression of pathology in the discriminator rather than an expression of inadequacy in himself. Not only is a basic change in Negro self-evaluation emerging, but the instrumental value of *claiming* self-devaluation no longer secures its historical purpose. McDonald and Gynther, using discrepancy between self and ideal-self as a measure of self-esteem, found that the self-esteem of black subjects was higher on average than that of their white peers, and Powers found that black students were not significantly lower on any of the self-perception scales and in fact were higher than non-Jewish whites in self-concept scores. Powers also doubts the hypothesis that when black children become part of an integrated school their self-concepts diminish. Soares and Soares (1969) concluded that disadvantaged children do not necessarily reflect negative self-perceptions or lower self-esteem than advantaged children.

We are able to be cautiously optimistic about levels of self-esteem in minority groups, on the basis of the last paragraph and on recently published surveys of research in this area. It is necessary to emphasize though the importance of noting defensive high self-esteem in minority groups and that in a substantial proportion of individuals progress towards resolution of conflict is absent. Detailed case histories of adolescents such as in Weinreich (1979) will allow more meaningful interpretation of self-esteem in minority groups. Samuels (1977) reports that a growing body of recent research of children from nursery school age to secondary school has indicated that the self-concept of non-white children seems to be more positive, whilst more recent studies of black students indicate higher self-concepts than those of whites. Studies which are controlled for social class seem to indicate that socio-economic status is a more significant factor in determining self-concept than race, and this seems to be especially so in academic aspects of self-concept. St. John (1975), in reviewing work on the desegregation of USA schools and its results on self-concept, concluded that in the long run desegregation was usually found to be associated with higher self-esteem after a transitory negative or mixed effect on scores. Coopersmith (1975), summarizing the considerable American research, noted the reverse of earlier trends for blacks to have lower self-esteem than whites, and that this is noticeably so 'as long as the child stays within an environment in which his culture is in a majority'. The implication of the quotation is the need for schools and society to maintain the esteem of individuals who move out of their own culture. Fortunately, after an instructive literature review, Bagley *et al.* (1979) conclude that self-esteem is derived from a variety of sources and that poor self-esteem is reversible both by counselling and by favourable shifts in social conditions.

The Handicapped Child

The self-concept of the handicapped child is a seriously under-researched area where the results of work to date are contradictory and inconclusive. Lawrence and Winschel (1973) pointed out the unsatisfactory nature of much existing research and the need for more longitudinal studies and longer periods of therapy and follow-up. Nevertheless, their review of research on the self-concept of the retarded child is a valuable pointer forward for future researchers. David Thomas (1978) reports that research with physically handicapped children appears to be more consistent and surveys studies of children with haemophilic condition, cerebral palsy, and visual handicap. Self-concepts are believed to act as mediators between physical status and perception of stress, parental influence on self-concept was important, the degree of self-esteem increased as the degree of disability decreased, and, as might be expected, handicapped children saw themselves as physically inadequate, had fewer close relationships and fewer opportunities for social participation. This book and 'The Psychology of Handicap' (Shakespeare, 1975) provide useful discussions on self-concepts and handicapped children. Investigations on the self-concept of handicapped and retarded children are urgent given the need not only to develop greater feelings of worth but especially to avoid any instances of extremely negative self-deprecation.

Disagreement exists on the school placement of handicapped children and whether handicapped children benefit psychologically by being educated together with 'normal' children. The importance of work in this area is highlighted by the Warnock Report (1978) with its plea for ending the acute distinction between handicapped and non-handicapped children by integrating the handicapped child into ordinary schools. At the same time much needs to be done about the provision for the pre-school child and studies of self-concept in pre-school handicapped children should be encouraged. Numerous studies have attempted to compare the self-concept of retarded children in special classes with those placed in ordinary schools where their classmates are of low academic ability like themselves. The evidence is equivocal and in studies surveyed by Robinson and Robinson (1976) in the USA, some research observed that children in special classes had lower self-concepts, some investigations showed no differences; and some demonstrated higher self-concepts in special class students. One problem, not always mentioned in research reports, is the abundant evidence of individual differences amongst retarded children and the obvious need for self-concept researchers to plan more longitudinal studies and evaluate more single case studies in this area. The variety of individual responses to handicap is noted in Litman (1962) with reference to the relationship between self-concept and medical treatment. The author quotes a seventeen-year-old male polio quadraplegic. He was intelligent, energetic, extremely well motivated. Throughout treatment he attempted to devise various procedures to assist his own case. His conception of self was extremely favourable, and it is significant that family and friends accepted him as a useful member of the community and showed great interest in his progress and his plans for the future. Another interesting study is cited in Wolff (1969) with the case of John aged seven with a mild cerebral palsy. The parents and teachers knew his muscular difficulty but he did not. He was aware only of his poor performance and criticism from others and he was anxious because his self-esteem was low. The same author interestingly discusses self-esteem with reference to children under stress.

A number of studies examine the self-concept of children with learning problems and insofar as these refer to particular problems of the educational system they are examined in the final chapter of this book with reference to school organization and self-concept.

Chapter 5

Self-concept and Achievement

Any research on achievement in school and college must take account of the fact that learning performance is affected not only by levels of intelligence but also by personality and that the teacher planning to get the best out of his or her pupils will take account of differences in personality as expressed through self-concept. The pupil or student will have a self-perception of success or failure which will determine his motivation to achieve. The dynamics of the relationship between self-concept and achievement has been theorized about or examined empirically by a number of scholars and earlier work is well documented by Purkey (1970) and has been more recently discussed by Nash (1976) and Burns (1977). The latter two writers, however, in spite of their avowed intention, cover a wider brief than just achievement in their relatively short accounts. The present chapter, therefore, seeks to fit its subject into theoretical perspective and then to outline research under the broad headings of correlational studies and achievement characteristics. In addition we shall examine two areas in greater depth – the well-known studies of Brookover and his associates, and the sparse literature on self-concept and creativity. Finally, we look at the self-concepts of teachers.

Theoretical Perspective

Achievement in school may be seen either in the narrow sense of success in a narrow range of subjects in which an individual is interested or in the wider sense of the pupil's overall achievement motivation. In the former sense pupils will work at subjects which they see as instrumentally important for them in reaching desired goals, and if a person considers a given school subject particularly valuable to him for his desired work, career, or leisure ambitions then failure in that subject will devalue his opinion of his ability in that area. Such failure will tend to lower his rating of his ability in other capacities and may indeed lower his whole self-esteem. Where failure in a subject not deemed important occurs then failure in that area has no such harmful effect because it will not affect his other self-evaluations. It seems reasonable that a pupil's self-concept characteristics will play a role in his reactions to success and failure. In particular, children who have generally poor self-regard may react to failure or stressful school tasks with greater anxiety than would pupils who have generally high self-regard. Theoretical and research evidence for such views is well documented in Diggory and Magaziner (1959), and in the well designed study of Solley and Stagner (1956) where subjects with poor self-regard showed less accuracy and speed in problem solving tasks, showed more physiological indicators of anxiety, and, when the task induced failure or threat of failure, made comments about their selves rather than about the task in hand.

Overall achievement motivation may be defined as the wish shown by an individual to satisfy his or her needs to satisfy drives to know and understand, to acquire feelings of personal adequacy, and to receive approval from others as part of a desire to master his or her environment. The theory of achievement motivation is learned under conditions which simultaneously teach a sense of self. Not surprisingly, therefore, there is widespread evidence that work on self-concept and school achievement makes theoretical sense in the light of this theory, and indeed makes theoretical sense when looked at in terms of general motivation theory, and when the self sentiment is seen as an integrator of motives (Cattell *et al.*, 1966). Different levels of achievement motivation lead to differential responses to success or failure and Kleinke (1978) records that students with low motivation for achievement tend to attribute their failure to a low level of ability, whilst students with high motivation for achievement tend to attribute their failure to a low level of ability, whilst students with high motivation for achievement tend to attribute their failure to a lack of effort on their part. Fitch (1970) noted that high self-esteem subjects internalized their successes but not their failures; low self-esteem students tend to internalize both success and failure. It should be remembered that fear of failure can itself be a motivating factor in achievement, though some writers suspect that fear of failure is independent of achievement motivation. It is noted, too, that some people with high self-esteem avoid experiences which threaten that self-esteem. Other individuals are afraid of success for various reasons, either because they see the cost of success as greater than the reward or believe that successful people are not necessarily happy or socially accepted. People who see themselves as only happy when doing better than others, who place high value on their own efforts, and believe achievement commands respect, demonstrate positive attitudes towards success. Those particularly interested in fear of failure are referred to Birney, Burdick and Teevan (1969).

Virtually all the research on abilities and personality leads one to believe that the key factor in educational attainment is that pupils must repeatedly experience success in school. This builds appropriate abilities, study habits, attitudes and values and minimizes those factors that inhibit successful performance. This is not to turn all our geese into swans and swans learn from the occasional failure. It is simply to argue, as in Covington and Beery (1976), that self-esteem is not something separate from performance but rather integral to it. It is through achievement that academic self-confidence grows, and increased confidence in turn promotes achievement through inspiring further learning. In short, confidence and competence must increase together for either of them to flower. Attaining high academic goals without a positive sense of self-worth can be disastrous for the pupil because for those who are insecure or low in self-esteem, anchoring a sense of worth on ability alone can be highly threatening and wrongly interpreted by the teacher. As the above authors write: 'For many youngsters expending effort is a threat because if they study hard and still fail, their ability becomes suspect. Consequently when students do not respond to teacher praise with increased effort, teachers become puzzled, sometimes angered, and may even feel betrayed. Though teachers are likely to regard such resistance as a lack of motivation, the student is usually far from unmotivated. To the contrary, he his highly motivated, but for the wrong reasons. He is trying to avoid a sense of failure and to protect his feelings of self-worth'.

Before looking at various studies examining the relationship between self-concept and achievement in some detail a general overview may be stated. Relationship between low self-concept and poor functioning in school is noted in Torshen (1971) and more positive self-concept related to higher academic achievement is seen in Caplin (1966). There is evidence from these and other studies that reported self-concept of ability is a better predictor of academic success than is the intelligence quotient (Morse, 1963; Haarer, 1964;

Lamy, 1965; Stenner and Katzenmeyer, 1976). Research in this general area suggest that realistic standards of excellence, elimination of excessive failure, the creation of conditions that maximize success, and intrinsic motivation all lead to a positive view of self and allow the pupil to profit from new learning experiences. This educational attainment in turn gives the pupil a sense of individual competence in his ability to reach those goals and gain those rewards valued by his reference group. Indeed, Weidman *et al.* (1972) found that educational attainment had stronger effects on self-evaluation of competence than either family income or occupational prestige and conclude that the impact of achievement on a wide range of attitudinal and behavioural factors needs further research.

Correlational Studies

Studies have indicated a positive correlation between self-concept and achievement (Coopersmith, 1959; Buck and Brown, 1962; Piers and Harris, 1964) and increasing underachievement is associated with increasingly poor self-concept (e.g. Black, 1974). The evidence is not always clear-cut however. Thomas (1971) found correlations between self-concept and attainment measures were negligible, while Bledsoe (1964) found his correlations were low to moderately positive. Phillips (1964) found the higher the achievement the higher the self-images of his college students, and Hishiki (1969) reports low and moderately positive correlations between self-concepts and achievements.

The field of self/ideal self discrepancy and achievement has seen a number of studies. Martire (1956) reported high discrepancies associated with high achievement motivation, while Remanis (1964) found that achievement motivation varied directly with the life goal/present status disparity. It would appear that motivational decline may be an important variable responsible for the low achievement of high self-ideal discrepancy groups. Deo and Sharma (1970) point out that few studies have tested the relationship of self-ideal discrepancy and achievement, and cite Perkins (1958), Mitchell (1959) and Turner and Vanderlippe (1958). Perkins reported no relationship over six months between changes in self-ideal congruence and changes in achievement; Mitchell showed that his self-rejecting group did as well in school as the self-accepting group; Turner and Vanderlippe obtained non-significant trends towards higher grade-point averages amongst subjects with high self-ideal congruence. However, the last two studies compared only extreme groups, and did not clarify the relationship when the middle group might differ significantly from the extremes. Deo and Sharma (1970) used a full range of 700 scores and indicated significant trends towards high school achievement as self-ideal discrepancy increases but showed that, after a certain limit, the increase becomes a handicap and achievement falls. Their results suggest that there is an optimum level of discrepancy score which is most conducive to high achievement. The self-contented lower scoring pupils appear to lack motivation while in the self-rejecting upper group the higher discrepancy involves a higher level of anxiety and a motivational decline which adversely affects achievement levels.

Achievement Characteristics

Numbers of studies examine the self-concepts of achievers and underachievers but unfortunately these studies lack common features of experimental design and common objectives. Mitchell (1959) looked at goal-setting behaviour as a function of self-acceptance, over- and underachievement and related personality variables. Four groups were identified: the self-acceptant underachiever, the self-acceptant overachiever, the self-rejectant underachiever, the self-rejectant overachiever. Each group was found to have different characteristics, e.g. the self-acceptant overachiever might be seen as the well-adjusted 'good' student. Often mediocre intellectually, such a pupil or student aspires to high grades, is hard working and expects to succeed. He or she obtains satisfaction through academic work but is not motivated by a strong sense of competition. He sees himself as mature, well-liked and not unduly nervous or anxious. Shaw, Edson and Bell (1960) found differences in self-concepts reported between achievers and underachievers, and the fact that male underachievers have rather stronger negative self-concepts as opposed to their female counterparts may help to explain why academic underachievement is primarily a male problem. The underachievers in this study describe themselves in words which would suggest likely failure at school, and in the Sarbin Adjective Checklist use adjectives such as fussy, confused, anxious, mischievous, easy going, and pleasure seeking. The data does not however indicate whether differences in self-concept are the causes of, or the results, of underachievement. Shaw and Alves (1963) point to a direct association between negative self-attitude and academic achievement, when ability levels are held to be equal.

Fink (1962b) compares achievement and underachievement amongst boys and girls and comes up with pen portraits of four groups in relation to self-concept. The girl achiever accepts herself, feels secure in the certainty that others will accept her, values hard work and learning, and sees herself as capable and smart. The underachieving girl appears poorly controlled and impulsive, is pleasure seeking, sees herself as socially alienated and a victim of circumstances, unhappy and misunderstood. The achieving boy accepts himself basically but not with the same degree of assurance displayed by the achieving girls. He accepts the values and goals of the dominant culture and appears to conform to the norms of that culture even in the face of inconsistencies. The underachieving boy is seen to be the most inadequate and immature of the four groups and appears alienated from society and perhaps from family. He does not hold to the ideals, values, and goals of the dominant cultural group. He tends to be pleasure seeking but so inadequate and passive that he never achieves his goals. Instead he complains of his powerlessness in a world dominated by power but is willing to concede that might makes right. Quimby (1967) confirms previous work relating low self-concept to underachievement and suggest that underachievers, especially girls, have unrealistic concepts. Storey and Clark (1968) report that underachievers are significantly more assertive and socially orientated than achievers, and that each group wishes to change in the direction of the other, underachievers being dissatisfied with their social assertiveness, achievers dissatisfied with concentration on academic work. The wish patterns of the underachiever may increase academic motivation, whilst those of the achiever may cause a fall off in attainment. This particular study is important in its recognition of the important interrelatedness of motivation, achievement and self-concept. Borislow (1962) concluded that, regardless of an intention to strive for scholastic achievement as a prime goal, students who underachieve scholastically have a poorer conception of themselves as students than do achievers subsequent to scholastic performance. Where students show themselves willing to strive for scholastic achievement as a prime goal, underachievers have a more pessimistic conception of themselves as students than do achievers prior to their actual scholastic achievement. Where scholastic achievement is a prime goal and where the student thinks well of himself as a student and does achieve scholastically, his general self-evaluation becomes more favourable. This is not true when scholastic achievement is not a prime goal. We are not told in this study whether the sample was of mixed or single sex and if mixed no attempt is made to control for sex. In that other researchers show men and women may well have differences in self-evaluation and in their motivation as students, the results outlined should be treated with some caution. Everett (1971) found differences in self-concept between high, medium and low academic achievers and gives a qualitative and descriptive study of those differences. McKenzie (1964) discovered that underachievers tended to internalize conflicts and were characterized as being impulsive, lacking long term motivation, and having low self-esteem.

Individuals of low self-esteem tend to reject success if they believe it later has to be reproduced and that they have an obligation to so repeat it (Jones, 1973; Mettee, 1971). People who are totally convinced of their negative self-picture tend to reject success, whereas individuals still uncertain of themselves, embrace success. Coopersmith (1967) identified two types of low esteem boys. One group not only doubted their self-worth but were also held in low regard by friends and teachers. Maracek and Mettee (1972) argue that this group of boys were certain of the validity of their negative self-appraisal because other boys confirmed it. They became caught in a self-concept of failure and gave up efforts to keep a sense of worth. The second group identified by Coopersmith were also low in self-esteem but were regarded highly by friends and teachers. These youngsters were far more successful in school because they were less certain about their potential and tried to lessen this uncertainty by working hard to prove their worth to themselves and others. These children may well become that species of pupil Covington and Beery (1976) refer to as 'over-strivers', where one's value must be proven constantly through an unbroken string of achievement. Studies such as these illustrate the need for parents and teachers to intervene as early as possible before failure at school becomes an ingrained lifestyle. As long as a boy or girl is uncertain about the cause of his failure, he may react favourably to praise and success. It is also extremely important not to treat all low-esteem students alike. It would be naive however not to realize that failure may also signal that personal limits of ability have been reached and that all the self-esteem and motivation in the world will not increase them.

This section concludes with a look at achievement-orientated individuals and the characteristics of people who are most inclined to experience success. Mukherjee (1969) found that achievement-orientated persons described themselves as ambitious, assertive, capable, confident, determined, enterprising, forceful, far-sighted, gracious, imaginative, dependent, industrious, and in other positive terms, while subjects who put a low level on achievement saw themselves as slow and submissive and in negative terms. Graduates with high achievement values tended to see themselves as more competent and sociable than graduate students having low achievement values. Achievement-orientated persons tended to show greater stability in opinion of self on dimensions such as sociability, flexibility, intellectual ability, emotional stability, and leadership. Kleinke (1978) has summarized the results of research on the self-perception of success and failure by outlining the characteristics of people who are most likely to experience success. People who are successful were generally raised on experiences of success. They were encouraged at home and in school to set high standards for themselves. Successful individuals have learned to interpret success as evidence of their ability. When successful people fail they are more likely than unsuccessful people to blame the failure on their lack of effort rather than on their lack of ability, and to seek out alternative responses that will help them overcome the failure. Success has all the characteristics of self-fulfilling prophecy and Hargreaves (1972) has suggested that the teacher's conception of the ability of the pupil, the child's own conception of his ability, and whether or not a boy or girl holds the teacher in high regard and values his or her conception of that boy or girl, all interact to bring about success. The pupils most likely to succeed are those seen as bright by teachers, who see themselves as bright, and who perceive the teacher as a significant other person in their lives.

Brookover and Associates

The various publications of Brookover and his fellow researchers at Michigan State University (Brookover *et al.*, 1962, 1964, 1965, 1967) are especially impressive studies of self-concept and achievement because of the substantial amount of work produced from a common methodological approach. The essential value of these studies is the explanation given of the causal relationship between self-concept and achievement. The conclusion reached by the research team is that self-concept of academic ability is a threshold variable, and they point out that low socio-economic status cannot be a wholly satisfactory explanation of low academic achievement because not all pupils of low social class do poorly in school any more than all middle and upper class children do well. Brookover suggests that below a certain level of ability children will not succeed in school whatever their social class or self-concept; but if the self-concept is low then not even very able middle class children will do well. Commenting on this hypothesis, Nash (1976) describes this as an attractive explanation because it helps to account for negative cases, where some disadvantaged pupils do very well in life. Brookover's work places self-concept as an intervening threshold variable between social class and achievement and places behaviour under the control of the individual. This view is not socially deterministic but still leaves room for the idea that an individual's life chances are heavily influenced by background variables like socio-economic status.

Following Nash, one can argue through the relationship between self-concept and achievement. A child with positive self-concept will want to maintain it, will probably regard the teacher as a significant other and wish to appear favourably in the eyes of the teacher, will want to live up to the expectations of the teacher, and in turn the reactions of the teacher towards that child are likely to become more favourable. His parents are likely to support the child and he or she will tend to be friendly with similar children. In contrast, the boy or girl with a poor view of his or her school abilities will tend to perform poorly in the classroom. There seem to be two possibilities. The child may be ashamed of his low ability and might even despair, or he may want to protect himself from further disparagement by maintaining his poor academic self-concept (it could maintain him in his friendships, etc.) ignoring his teacher's opinions, and reinforcing his teacher's perception of him as not trying very hard at school work. His parents may care little about, or be hostile towards, school and he will tend to make friends with other low achievers like himself. As we have seen earlier in this chapter, all these linkages can be supported by research studies. These are very tightly knit circles and they revolve as much by the perceptions and expectations people hold about each other as by their actual behaviour.

Creativity

The literature on self-concept and creativity is sparse and the two major studies remain Mackinnon (1963) and Hudson (1968). Four smaller scale studies of some importance are Rivlin (1959), Trezise (1967), Schaefer (1969) and Maw and Maw (1970). The first named of these four authors attempted to examine the validity of certain assumptions regarding the creative personality in American high school students. Creative students emerged as rather sociable individuals, evaluating themselves as more confident in their relationships with people, and more popular and creative as viewed by their friends than were their non-creative fellow students. The general conclusion reached by Rivlin was that the creative student did not differ in overall self-attitudes from the non-creative. Sex differences in self-concept are found by Trezise in a descriptive study of the life styles of a group of creative adolescents. Creative girls as compared with non-creative girls tended to see themselves more unfavourably than did creative boys as compared with non-creative boys. Moreover, creative girls tended to be introspective and interested in self-understanding than were creative boys. Schaefer concluded that a person's self-image played a major part in motivating him towards creative achievement, and found that creative adolescents (compared with a control group of non-creative pupils) exhibited complexity and reconciliation of opposites, impulsivity and craving for novelty, autonomy, and self-assertion. Maw and Maw look at the self-concepts of boys who exhibit high or low levels of curiosity. As curiosity is only one strand of the creative personality and as the middle level of curiosity is ignored this study has its limitations, but deserves to be replicated. High curiosity boys scored significantly higher on tests of self-reliance, sense of personal worth, sense of personal freedom, feeling of belonging, strong self-sentiment, lack of withdrawing tendencies, ego strength and total personal adjustment. Low curiosity boys revealed more prejudice than high curiosity boys, had lower feelings of social responsibility, and were more intolerant of others, than were boys with high curiosity. Boys with low self-concepts may expect failure and avoid curiosity in situations where failure might occur. Conversely, in their lack of curiosity, low curiosity boys miss out on those experiences which help develop high levels of self-esteem. One must also add that background variables in the development of boys with low curiosity which create poor concepts of self may also be the conditions promoting low curiosity.

Mackinnon, primarily a brilliant researcher into creativity, has produced a composite self-image of the creative architect. In summary, architects, regardless of the level of their creativeness, tend to think well of themselves, but the quality of the self-concept of highly creative architects differs from that of their less creative colleagues. Where the former group more often stress their inventiveness, independence, and individuality, and their enthusiasm, determination, and industry, their less creative colleagues are impressed by their own virtue and good character and by their rationality and sympathetic concern for other people. The author points out that in focusing upon images of the self many traits and dispositions which clearly determine the limits within which one is creative have been ignored. In any complete discussion of the determinants of creativity their role would have to be considered yet the relationships which have been demonstrated between the self-images and creativity of architects stand in their own right as compelling testimony to the dynamic character of the self in determining the person that any individual becomes.

As part of a larger study Hudson (1968) looked at the differing self-perceptions of convergent and divergent thinkers, where the latter group may be equated with creative thinkers if we accept the over-simplified equation of divergent thinking with creative or open-ended thought processes. Consistent differences emerge in the study and convergers seem less likely than divergers to differentiate between Actual and Ideal Self; between Perceived and Future Self; and between Actual and Future Self. Overall, divergers are almost exactly twice as likely as convergers to differentiate between the various selves; but easily the largest of these differences is that between Actual and Future Self. This suggests that by middle adolescence, convergers are much more settled than divergers about the kind of person they expect to become. Hudson goes on to link this with curriculum choices and argues that it may well be that subjects like physical science attract strongly boys who see relatively little change in their own character and way of life. Also, convergers tend to accept the cultural myths of the arts and sciences uncritically. Among divergers, this acceptance is only partial. In conclusion it seemed to the author that in a highly competitive and stratified school, boys are saturated with convergent reasoning and pupils assume that convergence and the ability to do well in examinations are one and the same; and the more successful they are the more perceptive about each other's powers of convergent reasoning they become. Conversely, the more successful they are the less sensitive they become to each other's capacity to diverge.

The two fields of self-concept and creativity research bristle with similar theoretical and methodological problems but increasing research into the relationships between the two variables is very necessary if we are to make the best use of the creative talent in our schools. We can only be satisfied with the present level of research if we equate creativity with high intelligence but the continuing investigations of creativity show that such an equation would be a gross oversimplification.

The Self-concepts of Teachers

Thomas (1973) commented that though the teacher has an important influence on the child's self-concept, the self-concepts of teachers themselves had received scant attention and the only reference given in the bibliography was to Phillips (1964), a study of the self-concepts of selected groups of training college students in relationship to other variables in the teacher training situation. Simpson (1966) devoted a chapter to the importance of self-concept of the teacher and emphasized that the teacher's self-perception is strongly influential in determining his classroom behaviour and attitudes but little in his analysis was based on empirical research directly related to self-concept and contributed more to a philosophy of teaching than to a psychology of teacher self-concept. Walberg (1967) produced an interesting study looking at self-concepts of prospective teachers of different religious affiliations. Catholics were more rigid, authoritarian and categorical than either Jews or Protestants. Atheists and agnostics appeared less rigid and authoritarian. Jews rated themselves highest on self-concept scales possibly because teacher and scholar have had high positions in Jewish culture.

Such empirical studies were an exception but in the last decade there has been a growing interest in teacher self-concept in relation to such variables as motivation, adjustment to teaching, teaching style, teaching characteristics, and choice of teaching as a profession. The research has little in common methodologically and I propose in this final section to briefly outline the findings and comment on them.

Cohen *et al.* (1973) examined a sample of 520 College of Education students who completed a need for achievement scale together with a semantic differential scale of self-image. Both males and females who were identified as high on need for achievement were found to hold self-images ('ambitious', 'hard-working', 'individualistic', etc.) consistent with a desire to succeed professionally and academically. Though this research is primarily one on achievement motivation it suggests a fruitful field for further studies, particularly those of a longitudinal nature where the reported sex differences could be more closely examined. An Australian study reported by Noad (1979) finds that self-concept and educational attitudes were related to the motivation of the student teacher. It confirms the belief that a student teacher's behaviour may be seen as the result of interacting emotional factors and reinforces the need for further data in this area. Indeed the author suggests screening procedures on entry to the teaching profession where information on a candidate's concept of self might be used as a possible predictor of future success in the classroom. This would seem logical in that the self-concepts of student teachers would play a part in influencing their behaviour as teachers and determine the results of their teaching. When motivated by needs for self-actualization the teacher would create a role which would provide outlets for personal growth, achievement, and satisfaction. This role creation would increase professional self-esteem and Doherty and Parker (1977) argue persuasively that self-esteem is an important factor in teaching behaviour for the social context of the school and classroom demands objective and realistic appreciation of the feelings and behaviour of other people. Since the self-esteem of the perceiver has an important influence upon this appreciation it is important that the self-esteem of student teachers be examined carefully with a view to appropriate professional socialization. Crane (1974) found empirical support for his hypothesis that there is a significant relationship between attitudes towards acceptance of self and others and adjustment to teaching, and this finding is of major practical importance given the wastage rate in the teaching profession. Three groups of student teachers were identified: students who appeared to be well adjusted to the course and to teaching; those who had seriously considered withdrawing from the course and were less well adjusted; students who were unable to adjust and had withdrawn from the course. The third group had significantly poorer opinions of themselves and others than the groups still in college and one wonders if the selection procedures suggested by Noad (1979) would have blocked admission to college for these students in the first instance and avoided even further lowering their self-esteem through their self-admitted failure in career choice. Crane's research does suggest that those students who show a high degree of self-acceptance and acceptance of others are those who will settle successfully in a teaching career. Burns (1976) has produced an important paper investigating whether attitudes to self and to others related to preferred teaching approaches on a continuum from traditional to progressive methods of teaching. He found that those teachers who prefer a personalized unstructured teaching context generally evaluate and accept themselves and others in a positive fashion. Those teachers who prefer more formal, structured and less personalized approaches, tend also to possess less favourable attitudes to themselves and to other people. Thus the self-concept would seem to be a major factor influencing preferred teaching styles in that those with low self and other attitudes are more likely to adopt teaching methods which defend their vulnerable personality structure. In view of the increasing evidence of stress in the teaching profession the relationship between teacher self-concept and teacher health would be a worthwhile subject for further research. One would expect such research to confirm the clinical picture that people are happier, more productive, more effective, and emotionally more balanced when able to evaluate themselves in positive terms. Trowbridge (1973), like Burns, is a pioneer attempt to relate the self-concept to the actual practice of teaching. She showed that teachers with lower self-concepts talk more and allow their pupils to talk less and that they spent almost twice as much time on routine matters than did teachers with high self-concepts, the latter group delegating routine matters to individual youngsters, leaving teacher and class free to pursue thinking and learning activities. The high self-esteem group were also found to use divergent and evaluative thought more whilst the less positive a teacher's self-concept, the more likely she was to use memory and convergent thinking with her class. This has obvious implications for the teaching of creativity in the classroom and attempts to strengthen teacher self-concept may well encourage a teaching style more likely to reward and encourage giftedness. It is important when considering teaching style to also take account of age and sex differences in a teacher's self-concept and attitude to education. For example, Kniveton (1976) found that young female teachers and older male teachers had less positive perceptions than other groups and he comments on the need for careful consideration of the consequences of this for the teaching profession in terms of teacher effectiveness (Vonk, 1971).

Our last three studies look at some characteristics of different teacher groups. Trowbridge, as reported above, found no differences between teachers of different pupil age-ranges in relation to self-concept. However, it is a folklore view amongst many educationalists that teachers of younger children are more 'person' than 'subject' orientated. Bown, Fuller and Richek (1967) quote studies in support of this view and themselves confirm the lay and often professional perception of the elementary school teachers in comparison with their secondary school colleagues as 'feeling' individuals in relation to children able to offer warmth and help to the youngsters in their care. A more recent British study by Morgan and Dunn (1978) investigating student reasons for choosing teaching as a career confirms that on the whole reasons concerning children are given top priority and that students choose to be primary school teachers to meet tender-minded or idealistic needs. In terms of self-realization they liked access to a wide curriculum and certainly did not feel, in terms of self-concept, that primary school teaching as a career gave them low professional status or lack of importance. The study is interesting in that, contrary to some mythologies, the women teachers were relatively more tough-minded than the men about choosing primary teaching. It follows from the study that a useful way of looking at teacher self-concept might be based on a four part model of teacher as educator (children orientated), teacher as worker (job orientated), teacher as person, and teacher as teacher – the last two perhaps being more central to what we understand as self-concept. The generalized educational experience of teachers is likely to be a strong influence on the development of their self-concepts. Bernbaum (1973) has developed this view in a preliminary study of headmasters showing that the schools and university attended will affect associated self-concepts, e.g. one headmaster who had thought he would never become a head teacher because 'I mean I was at the University of Exeter and I thought all heads came from Oxford and Cambridge, and I thought if you didn't talk with a fancy accent you knew you would stand no chance'. It may well be, given this precedent, that the most fruitful way of investigating teacher self-concept is the in-depth interviewing of individuals and the careful sifting of individual self-reports. Much self-concept research began in this relatively 'soft' methodology, and in investigating previously unlooked at populations a return to less sophisticated approaches may yield better results than factor analyses by the score and computer print-outs by the yard.

Chapter 6

School Organization

As we have seen earlier in this book, all sorts of experiences in school will influence the development of self-concept in growing children and adolescents. In this final chapter we look only at the effects of school organization. It so happens that in recent years research into schools as organizations has been one of the growth points in educational studies. A part of that growth has concerned itself with research into streaming, the name given to the practice of dividing all the children of the same chronological age into separate teaching groups on the basis of general intellectual ability. Streaming and the self-concept is the first area looked at here, followed by some brief comment on 'open education'. I shall then consider those studies of special provision or special placement for exceptional children, and examine specially organized programmes of study and out-of-school activities. As the teacher will be seen to emerge as a major 'significant other' in the aetiology of pupil self-concept we will conclude with a general consideration of the influences of headteachers and teachers in the overall administrative organization of the school.

Streaming: Lunn and Ferri

Acland (1973) in a review of research on streaming in English primary schools has commented that teachers who refuse to stream children have justified their professional stand by arguing that non-streaming improved the self-concept of the pupils. This is a simplistic view of the relationship between streaming and self-concept. The facts are not that convenient, as a summary of the findings of Lunn (1970) and Ferri (1971) reveals.

The major research by Lunn was a longitudinal investigation of approximately 5,500 children through their junior school course in 72 schools. Thirty-six of these schools were streamed, thirty-six were not streamed. The findings in regard to attitudes to self were as follows: neither school organization nor types of teacher much affected the development of self-concept in children of above average ability, but it did affect the self-image growth of children of average and below average ability; children of average ability were especially influenced by teacher type in developing academic self-concept, and pupils who were taught by typical non-streamers in non-streamed schools were better off than their counterparts in streamed schools. The poorest self-concepts were held by pupils taught by 'typical streamers' in non-streamed schools. More boys of below average ability had a good academic self-image in streamed schools than in schools that were not streamed. In group discussions with pupils it became clear that the children saw the teacher as influencing their motivation, degree of confidence, and self-concept. Most children had a clear picture of their academic ability, and knowing his or her stream made a pupil fully aware of his ability relative to the rest of his age-group. A considerable number of children of poorer ability in non-streamed schools had poor self-concepts, were ashamed of not being clever and felt their teachers constantly compared them with bright members of the class. It is interesting that the more recent ethnological studies also show children learning different perceptions of their abilities and, for example, Blease (1978) in a small slice of lesson analysis clearly indicates a child learning that his replies are highly valued, while another pupil is learning that even when he has a useful contribution to make to the lesson the teacher ignores him and he might as well just not bother, thus simply confirming the teacher's view of him.

It would be possible to examine further the detailed findings of Lunn but let us move on to the follow up study by Ferri. This research looked at 815 children in non-streamed junior schools and 901 in streamed junior schools who were subsequently transferred to grammar, comprehensive and secondary modern schools. These were pupils from 14 matched pairs of streamed and non-streamed primary schools in the Lunn study. At 12+ the boys continued to display a more academic self-concept than the girls and brighter children again had a higher self-concept than duller ones. Girls of above average ability from both types of school had developed a poorer self-image. At below average ability level both boys and girls who had attended non-streamed schools had developed a more favourable self-concept. Children who went to grammar schools developed a poor self-image, while boys in comprehensive or secondary modern schools had improved their self-image. No significant change had taken place in self-concept scores of girls who transferred to non-selective schools. The author explains these findings as follows. The more able pupils, especially girls at grammar schools had gone from being top of their respective classes to compete with intellectual equals. They were no longer the brightest children in their class or school. But junior school boys of above average ability in general had shown a slight improvement. These findings suggest that it was the able boys who had gone to comprehensive schools who had improved their self-concepts. Given the full ability range of the comprehensive school those pupils of above average ability again found themselves either in a high stream or a high class position, according to the method or organization in the school. The improvement in self-concept shown by boys and girls of below average ability from non-streamed junior schools and reflected in the scores of boys in secondary modern schools might also be explained in terms of a change in relative position in school or class. These pupils had all been at or near bottom of the junior school class but in the restricted ability range of the secondary modern school a sizeable proportion of them were no longer captive in the very bottom ability group or stream.

I have spent some time on the two NFER researches because they are the major studies examining the relationship between streaming and self-concept. Indeed, as Roy Nash (1976) has commented, the researches demonstrate two significant relationships overlooked by earlier work. A teacher's beliefs about teaching affect the self-concepts of his or her pupils, and this factor is particularly detrimental when the teacher is required to teach in a context that is incompatible with his or her beliefs. Additionally the surveys show the importance of class position for the pupil's self-picture. 'It is not his actual ability that seems to matter so much as his ability as he compares it with others in his class. The self-concept of children transferred to grammar school does not rise – as one might reasonably have expected – but it drops as the children's standard of comparison rises.' (Nash)

Other Studies of Streaming

When the American scholar Dyson (1967) investigated the literature he could find only one study dealing with the effects of grouping procedures on self-concept and that was an inconclusive study by Mann (1960) which looked only at homogeneous groups of children. What Lunn, Ferri and Dyson really say is that regardless of grouping procedures in a school, high achievers report more positive self-concepts than those of low achievers. Success in school significantly influences the academic self-concept in a positive direction regardless of grouping procedures. What comes out in these studies are in those of Emmett (1959) and Thomas (1971, 1974b) is the importance of the classroom teacher and his relationship with the individual child. Stephen Wiseman, commenting in 1970, on the Lunn research, has confirmed this impression: 'Teachers are more important than organizational structure. A school may be "unstreamed" as far as pupil allocation to classes is concerned, but if it is staffed by "streaming teachers" the methods within the classroom and the effects on the children will be similar to those found in schools with a totally streamed structure and policy . . . the single most significant outcome of educational research in the last decade is this power of teacher attitude and teacher expectation'. This opinion is supported in my 1971 study (abstracted as Thomas 1974b) where, though there were differences in the structure of self-concept between pupils in the A, B and C streams of the primary school there was also a lack of significant difference between the streams in level of self-concept. It was concluded that this school as an institution encouraged a similar level of self-evaluation in all pupils. The overall organization of the school was democratic, pupils were given clearly defined and enforced limits of permissible behaviour, the teachers treated the pupils as individuals, and the teachers themselves had positive self-concepts. In brief the teaching climate of the whole school was the important factor.

Open School and Beyond School

The difficulty facing some children in school when they wish to enhance self-esteem is one of relative lack of freedom either for curriculum choice or for personal growth. In the USA the concepts of open schooling and open classrooms have been developed in an attempt to provide greater freedom for pupils. Open schooling allows children to develop their own methods of learning at their own rate of speed in areas of study of their own choosing. The teacher decides which activities and materials are available and fixes the ultimate goals for the child. Most open schools encourage discovery forms of learning and are non-graded. Cockerham and Blevins (1976) provide an operational definition of the open school as follows: a flexible learning environment with large open work areas surrounding a resource centre and library; information teaching methods; non-graded procedures; emphasis upon student decision making and responsibility. The research reported by these two authors supported the argument that open school students feel better about themselves, and in particular that open school experience had assisted the development of a positive attitude towards self among a group of Indian youths with a relatively negative self-image. Not all studies support the one just quoted. It is contradicted by Klass and Hodge (1978) who could find no difference in the self-concepts of their 350 seventh-grade students in Denver, Colorado, distributed between open format and traditional classrooms. Though more encouraging results indicating that increased self-esteem may arise from using alternative schools exist (Strathe and Hash, 1979), the general impression of Rathbone (1972) still holds true: there is a paucity of research on the merits of open education and that which is available provides inconsistent findings in relation to its affective impact on children. One of the reasons for the lack of consistency is an overdependence on the psychometric model in educational research. Another major reason is that open school settings vary widely in actual practice. We need careful studies of individual schools, both in the UK and USA, on the lines of either Lacey (1974) which, though using a psychometric approach, analysed in depth the effects on self-concepts, and teachers' views of students of the organizational changes in a single grammar school under a new headmaster compared to a previous head who had streamed and 'express' streamed, or the observational approach of King (1978) whose study of infant classrooms poses many questions on school organization and self-concept though that topic as such can only be inferred from the study. The approach of King used specifically in examination of self-concept and self-esteem could be very fruitfully adopted at all levels of education.

Bellaby (1974) has argued that hostility to school arises where the third year secondary school pupil's concept of his or her future status makes schooling seem irrelevant and where the staff of the school imposes what is on the whole a strict as opposed to a lax disciplinary regime. One result, at least in Britain, is that pupils either leave school completely as soon as legally possible or transfer to colleges of further education. The field of further education is in general badly researched and work on the self-concepts of students in further education is virtually totally absent. Two exceptions to this general rule are Sharp (1970) and Ratigan (1978, 1979), and both studies suggest further investigations. Sharp found that the FE students regarded themselves as substantially happier, livelier, and more mature than sixth formers but saw the latter as more intelligent and hard-working.

Sixth formers were seen as moderately conforming and FE students as rebellious. The sixth formers were also regarded as very much tidier than FE students but FE students were seen as more responsible. Other interesting findings are reported comparing FE students from different school backgrounds. The unpublished doctoral study by Ratigan is a first rate example of the use of case study material where the constant theme is the students' interview accounts of their using the move to college as an aid in the development of their self-concepts. Going to college was seen as helping to put the individual self in perspective and in attempting to establish self-identity the students can be seen as moving from an environment where the possibility of establishing self-identity was not seen as existing, or only in a limited form, to one where such a possibility was more likely to occur.

Special Classes and Special Schools

Whether to segregate children with special problems from the normal school population has always been a matter of contention. The researchers in this area are themselves contradictory and have been reviewed comprehensively by Lawrence and Winschel (1973). Andrews (1966) in looking at the self-concept of pupils with learning difficulties quoted many studies which pointed to the tendency for schools to devalue the self in children with slow mental development, and that children of lower than average ability have more difficulty than other children in gaining feelings of achievement and in developing favourable self attitudes. He quotes an unpublished New Zealand study by Higgins (1962) who found a significant difference between the self-concepts of mental retardates in a special school and those in a normal school. The retarded pupils in the normal school saw themselves in much more negative terms, a finding supported by Lewis (1971) who studied the self-concept of 100 educationally subnormal boys aged twelve – fifteen years, educated in day special schools. A control group of academically average comprehensive school-boys were matched for age and LEA locality. Lewis found that significantly higher mean self-concept scores were obtained by the ESN boys than by the control group and that the earlier children were admitted to day special schools the higher were their self-concept scores. Lewis believed that the low level of self-regard amongst average comprehensive school-boys was caused by the polarization of teacher interests to extremes of ability in the comprehensive school. The average or 'Newsom' child suffers from a lack of concern. The special schools, on the other hand, met the emotional and social needs of their pupils because of closer personal relationships between teachers and taught. One suspects that a key factor here is the more favourable teacher-pupil ratio in the special school, and support for this interpretation comes from two papers by Lawrence (1971, 1972). In the 1971 study Lawrence aimed to investigate the effects on reading attainment of individual personal counselling compared with the results obtained by a traditional programme of remedial teaching, and to consider the association between certain personality characteristics and reading retardation. Four groups each containing twelve primary school children retarded in reading were matched and each group subjected to different treatments. At the conclusion of a six month period the counselled group showed a significant rise in reading attainment over all other groups, together with improved self-images. In the 1972 study non-professional personnel working with retarded readers were shown to achieve the same results as those obtained in the previous study by the trained psychologists. Through counselling the children improved their image of themselves and regained much of their lost confidence. It is interesting that these non-professionals were abundant in emotional response and it raises serious questions about the selection and training of teachers and the organization of schools. However remedial programmes are organized, the key point is that made by Quicke (1975): 'the type of remedial programme recommended must be based on psychological needs which differ from one child to another'. This is true whether the course is counselling centred as in Lawrence (1973) or more technological and behavioural as in Parker (1969). We are here at the core of the problem: a trained teacher is not necessarily able to help the child in achieving more positive self-concepts for as Carl Rogers (1962) has written 'in a wide variety of professional work involving relationships with people, it is the quality of the interpersonal encounter with the client which is the most significant element in determining effectiveness'. In other words, it is the teacher as 'person' not the teacher as 'teacher' who counts in the classroom, and as Roy Nash (1973) has shown us the teacher as 'person' may quite unconsciously contribute to the child's poor image of himself. He tells us on page 85 of his important book, that the criteria for inclusion in the remedial class was not low ability but a completely unfavourable image in the eyes of the teacher. The children who made up the remedial class of twelve – thirteen year olds had been seen by their primary school teacher not only as dull and less capable, but as troublesome, badly behaved, passive, stolid, immature and lacking in confidence.

It is no surprise, if Nash is correct, that remedial classes often live up to their reputations and only serve to prove the teacher right! Some researchers would therefore argue for integration in the school rather than for segregation of children with learning problems. Meyerowitz (1962) in a study of 120 children of IQ 60 to 85 found that the insensitivity to status usually attributed to young retardates was not supported and that after one year's segregation the retarded children had developed a more negative self-concept than if left with their normal peers. The pupils had appeared not to have realized the compensatory nature of segregation in the school situation and were evaluating their selves on the basis of their failings not their strengths. Carroll (1967) showed that educably retarded children in a segregated setting showed less improvement in self-concept than if left in a partially integrated situation. Parmenter (1970) indicated that partially sighted children in a unit attached to a normal school had no significant difference in self-concept scores from a normal school group. He suggested that attachment to a normal school gave the pupils opportunity for academic achievement and encouraged the development of an adequate self-concept. The essential argument here is once again to regard pupils as persons and to individualize our teaching from the 'perspective of the personal' as Professor Ben Morris has termed it. Woods (1979) in a case study of a single school has suggested that 'real' selves were mostly not to be found, for either pupils or teachers, in the formal structure and programme of his school but in private areas and moments. He argued that pupils are well able to distinguish between personal and bureaucratic treatment of them and that teachers need to forge less 'role-bound' relationships with colleagues and pupils to counterbalance the worst effect of institutionalization. It is salutory to find that when a school task is speeded up or slowed down to accommodate able and less able children who are motivated, the results are beneficial in terms of self-concept (Storey, 1967). It would appear that the more we regard education as an institutional process and less a person-to-person process the more likely we are to depress self-concepts in children.

Studies continue on the placement of exceptional children and it is possible to assume widely divergent positions about the way that special class placement influences the self-esteem of pupils as, for example, is shown in Battle (1979). Some writers assume that segregation of these children tend to foster negative feelings of self-worth. Supporters, on the other hand, insist that the special class or special school environment, which is generally less competitive, reduces the anxieties and frustrations of boys and girls experiencing learning difficulties and, therefore, as a consequence, tends to stimulate the growth of self-worth. Each position is interesting and supported by evidence but, as so often in the self-concept field, far more empirical data is needed before a really balanced view of the affective effect of placement can be achieved.

Out of the Classroom

It is in an attempt to avoid institutional characteristics in schools that educators have encouraged out-of-school activities and courses of study outside school. Outward bound courses, summer camps, school holidays and exchanges abroad, Duke of Edinburgh award schemes, the Welsh League of Youth, are all attempts to personalize relationships between teacher and pupil or to contribute to the personal development of the growing self. How successful are such attempts in contributing to the growth of a positive self-concept? There are wide impressions of success. Objective data is provided by six studies amongst others and we shall look at them in publication order (Beker, 1960; Frankel, 1964; Clifford and Clifford, 1967; Payne *et al.*, 1970; Grabe 1976; and Yarworth and Gauthier, 1978).

Beker looked at the influence of school camping on the self-concepts of 14 school classes participating in five-day school camping programmes as part of their regular curriculum. In a well designed study a significant and marked positive changes in self-concept were shown by the campers. The control groups did not reflect these changes. The differences were even greater after a lapse of ten weeks than immediately after the camp experience suggesting the continuation of growth processes started at camp. Beker argued that if the specific elements in school camping experience that tend to promote growth of self-concepts can be identified the way might be opened for increasing the effectiveness of a variety of educational settings including the classrooms. The analysis of classroom behaviour is a growth area in educational psychology. It might well be extended beyond the walls of the school. Frankel's paper is a study of the effects of an American programme of advanced summer study on the self-concepts of academically talented high school students. Frankel showed that it was possible to design a curriculum which not only produced the expected academic learning but also built positive self-concepts in pupils. The self-concepts of Frankel's group showed significant gains in self-reliance and in development of special academic studies. Clifford and Clifford examined the self-concepts of a group of adolescent boys aged sixteen – twenty-one before and after survival training. The boys were enrolled in an outward bound school summer camp which aimed to build physical stamina and to push each individual to his physical limit. Overall changes in self-concept took place in the direction of increased self-worth and confidence and discrepancies between the self and the ideal-self were reduced. The thirty-six boys were in camp one month, from a variety of socio-economic backgrounds, represented all levels of educational attainment and included a mixture of racial and ethnic backgrounds. It should be pointed out that no control group was used and that the effects of survival training are not unidirectional – an examination of individual scores showed that some boys changed in a less positive direction. Payne and his co-authors looked at changes in the self-concepts of thirty-six male school leavers who participated in an Arctic expedition. Using a control group, unlike Clifford and Clifford, they revealed that those volunteering for the expedition were significantly more extrovert than the general population of students and that in those who took part there was a significant reduction in the discrepancy between self-description and ideal self-description by the end of the expedition. But there were differences in type of school attended and a suggestion that changes in self-concept occur in more than one way should encourage us to think more clearly about the dynamics of change within individuals as a result of experience of this sort. Grabe wanted to relate feelings of self-worth arising from school-sponsored activities to size of school attended by students. It was found that students in small schools were involved in more activities, confirming previous research which had shown that in small schools students experienced a greater sense of obligation to take part in activities. It is interesting that the lower self-concept scores were produced by pupils who felt that their own priorities were different from the expectations of the school. The psychological impact of being able to meet the pressures exerted by fellow pupils to participate in activities is important and Grabe proposes that feelings of personal worth are related to a student's ability to respond to the perceived demands of the school environment. A child from a small school may feel humiliated in his or her failure to be selected for an athletic team. Few children among the much larger numbers in a big school would be ridiculed by their school friends for such a failure. Yarworth and Gauthier (1978), in research with 459 students in Pennsylvania high schools reported significantly higher self-concept scores for pupils who participated in school activities than for those who did not; also noting that 38 per cent of the pupils joined in no out-of-class activities of any kind.

Studies such as the above relating self-esteem with participation in out-of-school, extra-curricular activities are valuable because they examine the psychological decisions made by a pupil on whether or not to join in such pursuits. Until recently major studies of adolescent behaviour and leisure concerned themselves only with the economic and social factors influencing involvement by pupils in these areas.

Administration

These last six studies are a far cry from the average school and classroom and the general findings from the earlier sections of this chapter point to the importance of the individual teacher. The majority of teachers are the employees of local education authorities. Foster (1964) showed that some educational administrations in the USA believed that the ordinary organization of a school predisposes people, especially those on the teaching level, to feel alienated from the school administration. They feel that attempts should be made to change the business and military style of school organization, with a hierarchy that puts both teachers and children in an inferior position where both are under pressure. This is hardly a climate calculated to improve teacher-pupil relationships and I have argued elsewhere (1971b) that it would appear that schools can produce leaders within themselves and that the communication structure of schools might be remodelled according to a theory of leadership, and thus help produce emergent leadership in our pupils and motivate them towards better learning. Only then will we get an overall organization in schools which provides what Foster calls a climate for self-improvement in our teachers. The headmaster and the teacher are central figures in promoting positive self-concepts in our pupils. A quarter of a century ago Taba (1955) pointed out in an important work on school culture that the head directly affects student behaviour. In an elementary school described by staff and researchers as rigid and authoritarian the children's values presented a picture of social distance, immature interpersonal perceptions and overemphasis on competition. The school presented what Sir Alec Clegg once called the shadow not the substance of true education, where pupils are regarded almost as pickets at the gates and teachers practice techniques of avoiding pupils and techniques to maintain teacher-pupil distance. Ira Gordon (1962) quotes a study by Maynard (1955) where in an investigation of principal, teacher and pupil behaviour in Tampa, Florida, it was found that if the principal was autocratic, pupils expressed unfavourable attitudes towards self, school, and fellow pupils. The more democratic the principal the more favourable the attitudes of pupils. Colin Palfrey in an important paper reveals the same pervading influence of the headteacher in two single sex secondary modern schools in which he taught. Palfrey (1973) identified a relationship between the headteacher's informal assessment of pupils and the pupils' self-image. The informal segregation of children into good and bad academic prospects was partly determined by the headteacher's beliefs about the pupil's potential achievement during and following their careers in school. By setting varying levels of expectation throughout the school the headteacher imposed a diminished self-concept upon a certain group of children. To a significant extent, therefore, the headteacher predetermines the child's developmental concept of himself not only as a pupil but as a person. Palfrey emphasizes the highly subjective nature of the headteacher's expectations and stresses the importance of school regimes and communication patterns, and the importance of the teachers who mediating between headteacher and pupils will themselves influence the child's image of his or her worth as an individual. In spite of the lack of experimental sophistication in this study the attempt to investigate the interaction between expectations of the headteacher and the pupils' self-image is a pioneering study in the UK.

The teacher is indeed the central influence in all we have said in this chapter and influences the development of self-concept, e.g. essay marks, report books, honours boards, competitive examinations, detention. For every child whose self is boosted is another whose worth is diminished. We are not yet as bad as America in this respect. Rosenberg wrote in 1965: 'No educational system in the world has so many examinations, or so emphasises grades as the American school system. Children are being constantly ranked and evaluated. The superior achievement of one child tends to debase the achievement of another'. The teacher has it in his power to avoid this debasement but it needs changes in the self-concepts of teachers to produce changes in the self-concept of children. It depends, as Purkey (1970) has pointed out, on what the teacher believes about himself, on what he believes about his pupils, on the attitude the teacher conveys to his pupils, on the atmosphere the teacher creates in school and classroom, on the sensitivity the teacher develops towards his pupils. Sidney Jourard writing in 'The Transparent Self' in 1964 puts these conditions into the words of the pupils: 'You can know me truly only if I let you, only if I want you to know me. If you want me to reveal myself just demonstrate your good will... Your will to employ your powers for my good, and not for my destruction'. Purkey, from collating various writings on self-concept, has produced guidelines of good teaching. They may seem impossible counsels of perfection calling for shifts in our concept of the role of the teacher which we feel impossible or unacceptable.

Conclusion

The gap between teacher and researcher has often seemed a widening one, partly because much research has seemed inapplicable to classroom problems and partly because the results seemed to reduce the teachers to feelings of helplessness in the face of massive variables like social class, genetics, and urbanization. But self-concept research is saying to the teacher: you are the backbone of the education system, not the social scientists or the armies of advisers and petty officialdom. The teacher is a force in the classroom and in the field of self-concept he is a force for good given he has the will to experiment and succeed. Teachers can enhance the self-concept through the provision of special curriculum materials (Combs and Gordon, 1967), through encouraging more personal and private talks with pupils in calm, supportive atmospheres avoiding dominating, threatening and sarcastic situations (Spaulding, 1963), through developing experimental curriculum projects designed to enhance self-worth in children (Crovetto *et al.*, 1967), and in general through becoming more person orientated in the classroom. The teaching subject and the person taught are the twin loci of the classroom world. Pederson (1966) has shown that the teacher has the ability to elevate the level of academic self-concept of the student through combinations of actions, gestures, comments, and other cues through which the pupil perceives his teacher's opinion of his ability to do homework and to realize educational aspirations. Teachers are able to internalize the behaviour felt appropriate to the healthy development of their pupils' self-concepts (Chadwick, 1967). Perkins (1958) provides evidence for the strength of these arguments: teachers in classrooms which have warm, acceptant relationships and those wherein teachers seek to understand children and to facilitate their growth and development seem to be situations enabling children to perceive the self-concepts of fellow pupils more objectively. Only in such teacher-pupil relationships can education provide experiences which would enable persons to become objective, open and acceptant to all experiences whether unfavourable or favourable to the self.

We are at the beginning again. Asked to consider our educational objectives. No one can deny that education is facing a crisis from economic and other factors. In America the deschoolers are in full cry, in Britain our city schools face problems of urban decay, teacher shortage, and increasing delinquency. There is little the teacher can do as teacher to improve society outside the gates of the school but a great deal that can be done to improve society inside the school. Not all our children are academic, by ability or inclination, but neither are all our pupils models of laziness and vandalism. Many are in need of help, perhaps more than we realize. Teachers are on the verge of a teaching revolution and teachers and pupils alike face the same depersonalizing threats of modern technological society. Only by seeing teaching as one of the helping professions and less an elitist procedure for purveying knowledge can we encourage a positive sense of worth not only in our pupils but in ourselves.

BIBLIOGRAPHY

ACLAND, H. (1973). 'Streaming in English Primary Schools', *Brit. J. Educ. Psychol.*, **43**,2, 151–161.

ADLER, A. (1930). 'Individual Psychology'. In: MURCHISON, C. *Psychologies of 1930.* Worcester, Massachusetts: Clark University Press.

AMATORA, S.M. (1945). 'Self-appraisal of children', *J. Educ. Res.* **39**, 25–32.

AMATORA, S.M. (1957). 'Developmental trends in pre-adolescence and in early adolescence in self-evaluation', *J. Genetic Psychol.*, **91**, 89–97.

ANASTASI, A. (1968). *Psychological Testing.* New York: Macmillan.

ANDREWS, R.J. (1966). 'The self-concept and pupils with learning difficulties', *The Slow Learning Child,* **13**,1, 47–54.

ARCHER, D. (1974). 'Power in groups: self-concept changes of powerful and powerless group members', *J. Applied Behavioural Sci.*, **10**,2, 208–21.

ARGYLE, M. (1969). *Social Interaction.* London: Methuen.

AXLINE, V.M. (1971). *Dibs: in search of self.* Harmondsworth: Penguin.

BAGLEY, C., BART, M. and WONG, J. (1978). 'Cognition and scholastic success in West Indian ten year olds in London: a comparative study', *Educ. Studies,* **4**,1, 7–17.

BAGLEY, C. and MALLICK, K. (1978). 'Development of a short form of the Piers-Harris self-concept scale', *Educ. Rev.*, **30**,3, 265–8.

BAGLEY, C., MALLICK, K. and VERMA, G.K. (1979). 'Pupil self-esteem: a study of black and white teenagers in British schools'. In: VERMA, G.K. and BAGLEY, C. *Race, Education and Identity.* London: Macmillan.

BAIN, R. (1936). 'The self-and-other words of the child', *Amer. J. Sociol.*, **41**, 767–75.

BATTLE, J. (1979). 'Self-esteem of students in regular and special classes', *Psych. Repts.*, **44**, 212–4.

BAUGHMAN, E.E. (1971). *Black Americans: a psychological analysis.* New York: Academic Press.

BAYNE, R. (1973). 'Real Self as a useful topic for first year psychology courses', *Bull. Brit. Psychol. Soc.,* **26**, 215–20.

BAYNE, R. (1974). 'Real Self: a reply to Laidlow', *Bull. Brit. Psychol. Soc.,* **27**, 497–9.

BAYNE, R. (1977). 'What does self mean in the term self-actualization', *Bull. Brit., Psychol. Soc.,* **30**, 213–4.

BEATTY, W.H. (1969). *Improving educational assessment and an inventory of measures of affective behavior.* Washington, D.C.: Association for Supervision and Curriculum Development. National Education Association.

BEKER, J. (1960). 'The influence of school camping on the self-concepts and social relationships of sixth grade school children', *J. of Educ. Psychol.,* **51**, 352–6.

BELLABY, P. (1974). 'The distribution of deviance among 13–14 year old students'. In: EGGLESTON, S.J. (Ed) *Contemporary Research in the Sociology of Education.* London: Methuen.

BERNBAUM, G. (1973). 'Headmasters and schools: some preliminary findings', *Sociol. Rev.,* **21**, 3.

BERTOCCI, P.A. (1945). 'The psychological self, the ego and the personality', *Psychol. Rev.,* **52**, 91–9.

BIRNEY, R.C., BURDICK, H. and TEEVAN, R.C. (1969). *Fear of Failure.* New York: Van Nostrand-Reinhold.

BLACK, F.W. (1974). 'Self-concept as related to achievement and age in learning-disabled children', *Child. Devopm.,* **45**, 1137–40.

BLEASE, D. (1978). 'Teachers' perceptions of slow learning children: an ethnographic study', *Res. Intelligence,* **4**,1, 39–42.

BLEDSOE, J.C. (1964). 'Self-concepts of children and their intelligence, achievement, and values', *J. Indiv. Psychol.,* **20**,1, 55–8.

BLEDSOE, J.C. and WIGGINS, R.G. (1973). 'Congruence of adolescent self-concepts and parents perceptions of adolescents self-concepts', *J. of Psychol.,* **83**, 131–6.

BLOOM, L. (1960). 'Self-concepts and social status in South Africa: a preliminary cross-cultural analysis', *J. Soc. Psychol.,* **51**, 103–12.

BLOOM, L. (1971). *The Social Psychology of Race Relations.* London: Allen & Unwin.

BOHAN, J.C. (1973). 'Age and sex differences in self-concept', *Adolescence,* **8**, 31, 379–84.

BORISLOW, B. (1962). 'Self evaluation and academic achievement', *J. of Counselling Psychol.* **9**, 246–54.

BOWN, O.H., FULLER, F.F. and RICHEK, H.G. (1967). 'A

comparison of self-perceptions of prospective elementary and secondary school teachers', *Psychol. in the Schools,* **4**, 21–4

BRODY, E.B. (1968). *Minority group adolescents in the United States.* Baltimore: Williams & Wilkins.

BROOKOVER, W.G., PATTERSON, A. and THOMAS, S. (1962). *The relationships of self-images to achievement in junior high school subjects.* Educational Publication Services, College of Education, Michigan State University.

BROOKOVER, W.B., THOMAS, S. and PATTERSON, A. (1964). 'Self concept of ability and school achievement', *Sociol. of Educ.,* **37**, 271–9.

BROOKOVER, W.B., LE PERE, J.M., HAMACHEK, D.E., SHAILER, T. and ERICKSON, E.L. (1965). *Self-concept of ability and school achievement 2.* Educational Research Series 31, Bureau of Educational Research Services, College of Education, Michigan State University.

BROOKOVER, W.B., ERICKSON, E.L. and JONES, L.M. (1967). *Self-concept of ability and school achievement 3.* Educational Publishing Services, College of Education, Michigan State University.

BROUGHTON, J.M. (1975). The development of natural epistemology in adolescence and early adulthood. Unpublished doctoral dissertation, Harvard University.

BROWNFAIN, J.J. (1952). 'Stability of the self-concept as a dimension of personality', *J. Abnorm. and Soc. Psychol.,* **47**, 597–606.

BUCK, M. and BROWN, R. (1962). 'The relationship between self-concept and the presence and absence of scholastic under-achievement', *J. of Clin. Psychol.,* **18**, 181–2.

BURNS, R.B. (1976). 'Preferred teaching approach in relation to self and other attitudes', *Durham Res. Rev.,* **36**, 1079–85.

BURNS, R.B. (1977). 'The self concept and its relevance to academic achievement'. In: CHILD, D. (Ed) *Readings in Psychology for the Teacher.* London: Holt, Rinehart & Winston.

BUROS, O.K. (1972). *Seventh Mental Measurements Yearbook.* New Jersey: Gryphon Press.

BUROS, O.K. (1974). *Tests in Print 2.* New Jersey: Gryphon Press.

BYRNE, E.M. (1978). *Women and Education.* London: Tavistock.

CALDEN, G., LUNDY, R.M. and SCHLAFER, R.J. (1959). 'Sex differences in body concepts', *J. Consult. Psychol.,* **23**, 378.

CALKINS, M.W. (1915). 'The self in scientific psychology', *Amer. J.*

Psychol., **26**, 495–524.

CAPLIN, M.D. (1966). 'The relationship between self-concept and academic achievement and between level of aspiration and academic achievement', *Dissertation Abstracts,* **27**, 979–A.

CARLSON, B.R. (1958). Parent-child relationships and self concept of children. Unpublished Ph.D. thesis, University of Michigan.

CARLSON, R. (1965). 'Stability and change in the adolescent's self-image', *Child Developm.,* **35**,3, 659–66.

CARROLL, A.W. (1967). 'The effects of segregated and partially segregated school programs on self-concept and academic achievement of educable mental retardates', *Exceptional Children,* **34**,2, 93–6.

CATTELL, R.B., SEALY, A.P. and SWENEY, A.P. (1966). 'What can personality and motivation source trait measurements add to the prediction of school achievement?', *Brit. J. Educ. Psychol.,* **36**, 3, 280–95.

CHADWICK, J.A. (1967). 'Some effects of increasing teachers knowledge of pupils' self-pictures', *Brit. J. Educ. Psychol.,* **37**,1, 129–31.

CLIFFORD, E. and CLIFFORD, M. (1967). 'Self-concepts before and after survival training', *Brit. J. Soc. Clin. Psychol.,* **6**, 241–8.

COCKERHAM, W.C. and BLEVINS, A.L. (1976). 'Open school versus traditional school: self-identification among native American and white adolescents', *Sociol. of Educ.,* **49**, 164–9.

COHEN, L., REID, I. and BOOTHROYD, K. (1973). 'Validation of the Mehrabian need for achievement scale with College of Education students', *Brit. J. Educ. Psychol.,* **43**,3, 269–77.

COHEN, L. (1976). *Educational Research in Classrooms and Schools: Manual of Materials and Methods.* London: Harper & Row.

COLEMAN, J.C. (1974). *Relationships in Adolescence.* London: Routledge & Kegan Paul.

COMBS, A.W. (1965). 'Teachers too are individuals'. In: HAMACHEK, D.E. (Ed) *The Self in Growth, Teaching and Learning.* Inglewood, New Jersey: Prentice Hall.

COMBS, A. and GORDON, I.J. (1967). Attitudes and behaviour of biological science curriculum study special materials classes in two Florida counties 1965–66. Final report to Biological Science Curriculum Study Director, Boulder, Colorado.

COOPERSMITH, S. (1959). 'A method for determining types of self-esteem', *J. Abnorm. and Soc. Psychol.,* **59**, 87–94.

COOPERSMITH, S. (1967). *The Antecedents of Self-Esteem.*

San Francisco: W.H. Freeman.

COOPERSMITH, S. (1975). 'Self-concept, race and education'. In: VERMA, G. and BAGLEY, C. (Eds) *Race and Education across Cultures.* London: Heinemann.

COOPERSMITH, S. and FELDMAN, R. (1974). 'Fostering a positive self-concept and high self-esteem in the classroom'. In: COOP, R.H. and WHITE, K. (Eds) *Psychological Concepts in the Classroom.* London: Harper & Row.

COVINGTON, M.W. and BEERY, R.G. (1976). *Self-worth and Learning.* New York: Holt, Rinehart & Winston.

COZBY, P.C. (1973). 'Self-disclosure: a literature review', *Psychol. Bull.,* **79**,2, 73–91.

CRAIN, R.L. and WEISMAN, C.S. (1972). *Discrimination, Personality and Achievement.* London: Seminar Press.

CRANE, C. (1974). 'Attitudes towards acceptance of self and others and adjustment to teaching', *Brit. J. Educ. Psychol.,* **44**, 1, 31–6.

CROVETTO, A.M., FISCHER, I.L. and BOUDREAUX, J.L. (1967). *The pre-school child and his self-image.* Division of Instruction and Division of Pupil Personnel, New Orleans Public Schools.

CROW, L.D. (1962). 'Excerpts from the diary of a teenage girl', *J. of Educ. Sociol.,* **36**, 26–9.

CROWNE, D.P. and STEPHENS, M.W. (1961). 'Self acceptance and self evaluative behaviour: a critique of methodology', *Psychol. Bull.,* **5**,8, 104–21.

CURTIS, B. and MAYS, W. (1978). *Phenomenology and Education.* London: Methuen.

DAVIDSON, H.H. and LANG, G. (1960). 'Children's perceptions of their teachers' feelings towards them related to self-perception, school achievement and behaviour', *J. Exper. Educ.,* **29**, 107–18.

DAVIE, R. (1972). 'The longitudinal approach', *Trends in Education,* **28**, 8–13.

DEO, P. and SHARMA, S. (1970). 'Self-ideal discrepancy and school achievement', *Adolescence,* **5**,19, 353–60.

DE SAUSSURE, J. (1971). 'Some complications in self-esteem regulation caused by using an archaic image of the self as an ideal'. *Internat. J. of Psychoanalysis,* **52**, 87–97.

DE VOS, G.A. (1968). 'Achievement and innovation in culture and personality'. In: NORBECK, E., PRICE-WILLIAMS, D. and McCORD, W.M. (Eds) *The Study of Personality.* New York: Holt, Rinehart & Winston.

DIGGORY, J.C. (1965). *Self-Evaluation: Concepts and Studies.* New York: Wiley.

DIGGORY, J.C. and MAGAZINER, D.E. (1959). 'Self-evaluation as a function of instrumentally relevant capacities', *Bull. Ass. Int. Psychol. Applied.*, **8**, 2–19.

DOHERTY, J. and PARKER, K. (1977). 'An investigation into the effect of certain selected variables on the self-esteem of a group of student teachers', *Educ. Rev.*, **29**,4, 307–15.

DREVER, J. (1964). *A Dictionary of Psychology.* Harmondsworth: Penguin.

DYSON, E. (1967). 'A study of ability grouping and self-concept', *J. Educ. Res.*, **60**, 403–5.

ELDER, G.H. (1968). 'The socialization of adolescents'. In: BORGATTA, E.F. and LAMBERT, W.L. (Eds) *Handbook of Personality Theory and Research.* Chicago: Rand McNally.

EMMETT, R.G. (1959). Psychological study of the self-concept amongst a group of pupils in a secondary modern school. Unpublished M.A. thesis, University of London.

ENGEL, M. (1959). 'The stability of the self-concept in adolescence', *J. Abnorm. and Soc. Psychol.*, **58**, 211–5.

ENGLISH, H.B. and ENGLISH, A.C. (1958). *A comprehensive dictionary of psychological and psychoanalytical terms.* London: Longmans.

EPPEL, E.M. and EPPEL, M. (1966). *Adolescents and Morality.* London: Routledge & Kegan Paul.

EVERETT, A.V. (1971). 'The self-concept of high, medium and low academic achievers', *Australian J. of Educ.*, **15**,3, 319–23.

FERRI, E. (1971). *Streaming: two years after.* Slough: NFER.

FINK, M.B. (1962a). 'Self-concept as it relates to academic under-achievement', *Calif. J. Educ. Res.*, **13**,2, 57–62.

FINK, M.B. (1962b). 'Objectification of data used in underachievement self-concept study', *Calif. J. Educ. Res.*, **13**,3, 105–13.

FISHER, S. (1970). *Body Experience in Fantasy and Behaviour.* New York: Appleton-Century-Crofts.

FISHER, S. and CLEVELAND, S.E. (1958). *Body Image and Personality.* New York: Van Nostrand.

FITCH, G. (1970). 'Effects of self-esteem, perceived performance, and choice on causal attributions', *J. of Personality and Soc. Psychol.*, **16**, 311–5.

FORDHAM, M. (1971). 'The empirical foundation and theories of the self in Jung's work'. In: The LIBRARY OF ANALYTICAL

PSYCHOLOGY I *Analytical Psychology: a Modern Science.* London: Heinemann.

FOSTER, R.L. (1964). 'A climate for self-improvement', *Educ. Leadership,* **21**, 275–76 and 321.

FRANKEL, E. (1964). 'Effects of a program of advanced summer study on the self-perceptions of academically talented high school students', *Exceptional Children,* **30**, 245–9.

FRANSELLA, F. and FROST, K. (1977). *On Being a Woman.* London: Tavistock.

FRAZIER, A. and LISONBEE, L.K. (1950). 'Adolescent concerns with physique', *School Rev.,* **50**, 397–405.

FREUD, S. (1949). *An Outline of Psychoanalysis.* London: Hogarth Press and Institute of Psychoanalysis.

GALDSTON, R. (1967). 'Adolescence and the function of self-consciousness', *Mental Hygiene,* **51**,2, 164–8.

GECAS, V. (1973). 'Self-conceptions of migrant and settled Mexican Americans', *Soc. Sci. Q.,* **54**,3, 579–96.

GERGEN, K.J. (1968). 'Personal consistency and presentation of self'. In: GORDON, C. and GERGEN, K.J. (Eds) *The Self in Social Interaction.* New York: Wiley.

GERGEN, K.J. (1971). *The Concept of Self.* New York: Holt, Rhinehart & Winston.

GLENCROSS, D.J. (1978). *Psychology and Sport.* New York: McGraw-Hill.

GOFFMAN, E. (1956). *The Presentation of Self in Everyday Life.* Edinburgh: Edinburgh University Press.

GOFFMAN, E. (1968). *Stigma.* Harmondsworth: Penguin.

GOFFMAN, E. (1969). *Behaviour in Public Places.* New York: Free Press.

GOODENOUGH, G.L. (1938). 'The use of pronouns by young children: a note on development of self-awareness', *J. Genetic Psychol.,* **52**, 333–46.

GOODMAN, M.E. (1964). *Race Awareness in Young Children.* New York: Collier-Macmillan.

GORDON, I.J. (1962). *Human Development from Birth through Adolescence.* New York: Harper & Row.

GORDON, I.J. (1969). 'The beginnings of self: the problem of the maturing environment', *Phi Delta Kappan,* **50**, 375–8.

GRABE, M. (1976). 'Big school, small school: impact of the high school environment', *Contemporary Educ. Psychol.,* **1**, 1, 20–5.

GRIFFITT, W.B. (1969). 'Personality similarity and self-concept as determinants of interpersonal attraction', *J. Soc. Psychol.*, **78**, 137–46.

GUNDERSON, E.K.E. (1965). 'Body size, self-evaluation and military effectiveness', *J. of Personality and Soc. Psychol.*, **2**, 902–6.

HAARER, D.L. (1964). 'A comparative study of self-concept of ability between institutionalized delinquent boys and non-delinquent boys enrolled in public schools', *Dissertation Abstracts*, **25**, 6410.

HALL, M. (1963). 'A study of the attitudes of adolescent girls to their own physical, intellectual, emotional and social development', *Educ. Res.*, **6**, 68–70.

HAMACHEK, D.E. (1965). *The self in growth, teaching, and learning*, Englewood Cliffs, New Jersey: Prentice Hall.

HARGREAVES, D.H. (1972). *Interpersonal Relations in Education*. London: Routledge & Kegan Paul.

HARRIS, C.M. (1971). 'Scholastic self-concept in early and middle adolescence', *Adolescence*, **6**, 23, 269–78.

HARRIS, D.B. (1973). *Involvement in Sport: a Somatopsychic Rationale for Physical Activity*. New York: Lea and Feberger.

HAVIGHURST, R.J., ROBINSON, M.Z. and DORR, M. (1946). 'The development of the ideal self in childhood and adolescence', *J. Educ. Res.*, **40**, 241–57.

HAVIGHURST, R.J. and MACDONALD, D.V. (1955). 'The development of the ideal self in New Zealand and American children', *J. Educ. Res.*, **49**, 263–73.

HEMMING, J. (1960). *Problems of Adolescent Girls*. London: Heinemann.

HEMMING, J. (1966). 'Struggle for self-fulfilment'. In: University College Faculty of Education (Ed) *Psychology of Adolescence*. University College Swansea, University of Wales.

HEMMING, J. (1971). 'The road to social maturity', *Trends in Educ.*, **22**, 18–26.

HEMMING, J. (1974). 'Emotional and moral aspects of adolescence'. In: PRINGLE, M.K. and VARMA, V.P. (Eds) *Advances in Educational Psychology 2*. London: University Press.

HERMAN, A.B. (1971). 'The effects of high school program choice on self-concept', *Alberta J. of Educ. Res.*, **17**,1, 13–9.

HIGGINS, L.C. (1962). Self-concepts of mentally retarded adolescents. Unpublished B. Litt. thesis, University of New England.

HILGARD, E.R. (1949). 'Human motives and the concept of the self', *Amer. Psychol.*, **4**, 374–82.

HILL, D. (1974). 'Adolescent attitudes among minority ethnic groups', *Educ. Rev.*, **27**,1, 45–51.

HILL, D. (1975). 'Personality factors among adolescents in minority groups', *Educ. Studies*, **1**, 43–54.

HISHIKI, P.C. (1969). 'The self-concepts of sixth grade girls of Mexican-American descent', *Calif. J. Educ. Res.*, **20**,2, 56–63.

HOGAN, E.O. and GREEN, R.L. (1971). 'Can teachers modify children's self-concepts?', *Teachers' College Record*, **72**,3, 423–7.

HOLLAND, R. (1977). *Self and Social Context.* London: Macmillan.

HORNEY, K. (1946). *Our Inner Conflicts.* London: Kegan Paul.

HUDSON, L. (1968). *Frames of Mind.* London: Methuen.

HURLOCK, E. (1974). 'Personality Development'. New York: McGraw Hill.

IBRAHIM, H. and MORRISON, W. (1976). 'Self-actualization and self-concept among athletes', *Res. Quarterly*, **47**, 1, 68–79.

Instructional Objectives Exchange (1972). *Measures of Self-Concept K-12.* Los Angeles: Instructional Objectives Exchange.

IRWIN, E.M. (1978). *Growing Pains: a study of teenage distress.* London: Woburn Press.

JACOBSON, E. (1965). *The Self and the Object World.* London: Hogarth Press.

JAMES, W. (1890). 'Principles of Psychology'. London: Macmillan.

JERSILD, A.T. (1951). 'Self-understanding in childhood and adolescence', *Amer. Psychol.*, **6**, 122–6.

JERSILD, A.T. (1952). *In Search of Self.* Columbia, New York: Teachers College.

JERVIS, F.M. (1959). 'The meaning of a positive self-concept', *J. of Clin. Psychol.*, **15**, 370–3.

JOHNSON, O.G. (1976). *Tests and Measurements in Child Development: Handbook 2.* San Francisco: Jossey-Bass.

JOHNSON, O.G. and BOMMARITO, J.W. (1971). *Tests and Measurement in Child Development: a Handbook.* San Francisco: Jossey-Bass.

JONES, M.C. and BAYLEY, N. (1950). 'Physical maturing among boys as related to behaviour', *J. of Educ. Psychol.*, **41**, 129–48.

JONES, M.C. and MUSSEN, P.H. (1958), 'Self-conceptions, motivations, and interpersonal attitudes of early and late-maturing girls', *Child Developm.*, **29**, 491–501.

JONES, S.C. (1973). 'Self and interpersonal evaluations: esteem theories versus consistency theories', *Psychol. Bull.*, **79**, 185–99.

JOURARD, S.M. (1964). *The Transparent Self.* New York: Van Nostrand.

JOURARD, S.M. and SECORD, P.F. (1954). 'Body-cathexis', *J. Consult. Psychol.,* **18**, 184.

JOURARD, S.M. and SECORD, P.F. (1955). 'Body-cathexis and the ideal female figure', *J. Abnorm. and Soc. Psychol.,* **50**, 243–6.

KAGAN, J., HOSKEN, B. and WATSON, S. (1961). 'Child's symbolic conceptualization of parents', *Child Developm.,* **32**,6, 625–36.

KANE, J.E. (1978). 'Letter to the Editor', *Health Educ. J.,* **37**,2, 164 In: KANE, J.E. (Ed) *Psychological Aspects of Physical Education and Sport.* London: Routledge & Kegan Paul.

KANE, J.E. (1978). 'Letter to the Editor', *Health Educ.,* **37**,2, 164 and 168.

KATZ, P. and ZIGLER, E. (1967). 'Self-image disparity: a developmental approach', *J. of Personality and Soc. Psychol.,* **5**, 186–95.

KELLY, G.A. (1955). *The Psychology of Personal Constructs I: a Theory of Personality.* New York: Norton.

KINCH, J.E. (1963). 'A formalized theory of the self-concept', *Amer. J. Sociol.,* **68**, 481–6.

KING, D.E.W. (1965). 'The self concept and personality development in a Kingston senior school'. Unpublished Dip.Ed. dissertation, University of the West Indies.

KING, R. (1978). *All Things Bright and Beautiful.* New York: Wiley.

KIPNIS, D.M. (1961). 'Changes in self concepts in relation to perception of others', *J. of Personality,* **21**, 449–65.

KLASS, W.H. and HODGE, S.E. (1978). 'Self-esteem in open and traditional classrooms', *J. of Educ. Psychol.,* **70**,5, 701–5.

KLEINKE, C.L. (1978). *Self-perception: the Psychology of Personal Awareness.* San Francisco: W.H. Freeman.

KNIVETON, B.H. (1976). 'Teacher attitudes and self-perceptions: an age and sex comparison', *Educ. Studies,* **2**,3, 185–91.

KOHN, A.R. and FIEDLER, F.E. (1961). 'Age and sex differences in perception of persons', *Sociometry,* **24**, 157–63.

KOHUT, H. (1971). *The Analysis of the Self.* New York: International Universities Press.

KOHUT, H. (1977). *The Restoration of the Self.* New York: International Universities Press.

KOSA, J., RACHIELE, L.D. and SCHOMMER, C.O. (1962). 'The self-image and performance of socially mobile college students', *J. Soc. Psychol.,* **56**, 301–16.

KUHN, M.H. and McPARTLAND, T.S. (1954). 'An empirical investigation of self-attitudes', *Amer. Sociol. Rev.,* **19**, 68–76.

LACEY, C. (1974). 'Destreaming in a pressured academic environment'. In: EGGLESTON, S.J. (Ed) *Contemporary Research in the Sociology of Education.* London: Methuen.

LAHIRY, M. (1960). A study of the attitudes of adolescent girls to their own physical, intellectual, emotional and social developments. Unpublished M.A. thesis, University of London.

LAIDLOW, J. (1974). 'Is Real Self a useful topic for first year psychology courses?', *Bull. Brit. Psychol. Soc.,* **27**, 129–31.

LAING, R.D. (1961). *Self and Others.* London: Tavistock.

LAMY, M.W. (1965). 'Relationships of self perception of early primary children to achievement in reading'. In: GORDON, I.J. (Ed) *Human Development: Readings in Research.* Glenview, Illinois: Scott Foresman.

LAWRENCE, D. (1971). 'The effects of counselling on retarded readers', *Educ. Res.,* **13**,2, 119–25.

LAWRENCE, D. (1972). 'Counselling of retarded readers by non-professionals', *Educ. Res.,* **15**,1, 48–51.

LAWRENCE, D. (1973). *Improved Reading through Counselling.* London: Ward Lock Educational.

LAWRENCE, E.A. and WINSCHEL, J.F. (1973). 'Self-concept and the retarded: research and issues', *Exceptional Children,* **39**,4, 310–9.

LECKY, P. (1945). *Self-consistency: a theory of personality.* New York: Island Press.

LEWIS, A.R.J. (1971). 'The self-concepts of adolescent ESN boys', *Brit. J. Educ. Psychol.,* **41**,2, 222–3.

LIPSITT, L.P. (1958). 'A self-concept scale for children and its relationship to the children's form of the Manifest Anxiety Scale', *Child Developm.,* **29**,4, 463–72.

LITMAN, T.J. (1962). 'Self-conception and physical rehabilitation'. In: ROSE, A.M. *Human Behaviour and Social Processes.* London: Routledge & Kegan Paul.

LIVESLEY, W.J. and BROMLEY, D.B. (1973). *Person Perception in Childhood and Adolescence.* London: Wiley.

LOEVINGER, J. (1976). *Ego Development.* San Francisco: Jossey-Bass.

LONG, B.H. (1969). 'Critique of Soares and Soares self-perceptions of culturally disadvantaged children', *Amer. Educ. Res. J.,* **6**, 710–1.

LOWE, C.M. (1961). 'The self-concept: fact or artefact', *Psychol. Bull.,* **58**, 325–36.

LUNN, J.C.B. (1970). *Streaming in the Primary School.* Slough: NFER.

MACKINNON, D.W. (1963). 'Creativity and images of the self'. In: WHITE, R.W. (Ed) *The Study of Lives.* New York: Prentice Hall.

MANN, M. (1960). 'What does ability grouping do to self-concept?', *Childhood Educ.,* **36**, 357–60.

MARACEK, J. and METTEE, D.R. (1972). 'Avoidance of continued success as a function of self-esteem, level of esteem certainty and responsibility for success', *J. of Personality and Soc. Psychol.,* **22**, 98–107.

MARTIRE, J.G. (1956). 'Relationships between self-concept and differences in strength and generality of achievement motivation', *J. of Personality,* **24**, 264–75.

MASLOW, A.H. (1954). *Motivation and Personality.* New York: Harper & Row.

MATTESON, R.W. (1956). 'Self-estimates of college freshman', *Personnel and Guidance J.,* **34**, 280–4.

MAW, W.H. and MAW, E.W. (1970). 'Self-concepts of high and low curiosity boys', *Child Developm.,* **41**, 123–9.

MAYNARD, H. (1955). Study of pupil human relations within a school as influenced by the principal's pattern of behaviour. Unpublished doctoral dissertation, University of Florida.

MEAD, G.H. (1934). *Mind, Self and Society.* Chicago: University of Chicago Press.

MENNINGER, W.C. (1953). 'Self-understanding for teachers', *Nat. Educ. Ass. J.,* **42**, 331–3.

METTEE, D.R. (1971). 'Rejection of unexpected success as a function of the negative consequences of accepting success', *J. of Personality and Soc. Psychol.,* **17**, 332–41.

MEYEROWITZ, J.H. (1962). 'Self-derogations in young retardates and special class placement', *Child Developm.,* **33**, 443–51.

MILLER, D.L. (1973). *George Herbert Mead.* Austin: University of Texas Press.

MILLER, E.L. (1967). A study of body image, its relationship to self-concept, anxiety, and certain social and physical variables in a selected group of Jamaican adolescents. Unpublished M.A. thesis, University of the West Indies.

MISCHEL, T. (1977). The Self: Psychological and Philosophical Issues. Oxford: Blackwell.

MISTRY, Z.D. (1960). A study of the self-picture as held by selected groups of adolescent girls prior to and after school-leaving age.

Unpublished M.A. thesis, University of London.
MITCHELL, J.V. (1959). 'Goal-setting behaviour as a function of self-acceptance, over- and under-achievement, and related personality variables', *J. Educ. Psychol.*, **59**, 93–104.
MORGAN, V. and DUNN, S. (1978). 'Why choose primary teaching', *Durham and Newcastle Res. Rev.*, **8**,41, 44–50.
MORLAND, J.K. (1966). 'A comparison of race awareness in northern and southern children', *Amer. J. of Orthopsychiatry*, **36**, 22–31.
MORSE, R.J. (1963). Self-concept of ability, significant others and school achievement of eighth-grade students: a comparative investigation of Negro and Caucasian students. Unpublished Masters thesis, Michigan Stage University.
MORSE, W.C. (1964). 'Self-concept in the school setting', *Childhood Educ.*, **41**, 195–8.
MOUSTAKAS, C.E. (1956). *The Self: Explorations in Personal Growth.* New York: Harper Bros.
MUKHERJEE, B.N. (1969). 'Some characteristics of the achievement-orientated person: implications for the teacher-learning process', *Int. J. Educ. Sci.*, **3**,3, 209–16.
MURPHY, G. (1947). *Personality.* New York: Harper Bros.
MUSA, K.E. and ROACH, M.E. (1973). 'Adolescent appearance and self-concept', *Adolescence*, **8**,31, 385–94.
MUSGROVE, F. (1969). 'Self-concepts and occupational identities', *Universities Quarterly*, **23**,3, 333–44.
MUSSEN, P.H. and BOUTOURLINE-YOUNG, H. (1964). 'Relationships between rate of physical maturing and personality among boys of Italian descent', *Vita Humana*, **7**, 186–200.
MUSSEN, P.H. and JONES, M.C. (1957). 'Self-conceptions, motivations and interpersonal attitudes of late and early maturing boys', *Child Developm.*, **28**, 243–56.
McCLELLAND, D.C., ATKINSON, J.W., CLARK, R.A. and LOWELL, E.L. (1953). *The Achievement Motive.* New York: Appleton-Century-Crofts.
McDONALD, R.L. and GYNTHER, M.D. (1965). 'Relationship of self and ideal-self descriptions with sex, race, and class in southern adolescents', *J. of Personality and Soc. Psychol.*, **1**, 85–8.
McKENZIE, J.D. (1964). 'The dynamics of deviant achievement', *Personality and Guidance J.*, **42**, 683–6.
McNAMARA, D. (1971). 'The wheel: an alternative instrument for

collecting semantic type data', *Brit. J. Educ. Psychol.*, **41**,1, 99–101.

NASH, R. (1973). *Classrooms Observed.* London: Routledge & Kegan Paul.

NASH, R. (1976). 'Teacher Expectations and Pupil Learning'. London: Routledge and Kegan Paul.

NATIONAL FOUNDATION FOR EDUCATIONAL RESEARCH (1973, 1976). *Register of Questionnaires and Attitude Scales.* Slough: NFER.

NOAD, B. (1979). 'Maslow needs hierarchy related to educational attitudes and self-concepts of elementary student teachers', *Educ. Rev.* **31**,1, 51–7.

OFFER, D. (1969). *The Psychological World of the Teenager.* New York: Basic Books.

OLASEHINDE, M.O. (1972). 'The development of the ideal self in some Western Nigerian school children', *Educ. Rev.*, **25**,1, 61–71.

ORPEN, C. (1972). 'The wheel and the table: the relative merits of two alternative instruments for collecting semantic type data', *Brit. J. Educ. Psychol.*, **42**,1, 86–7.

OSGOOD, C.E., SUCI, G.J. and TANNENBAUM, P.H. (1957). *The Measurement of Meaning.* Urbana: University of Illinois Press.

PALFREY, C.F. (1973). 'Headteachers' expectations and their pupils' self-concepts', *Educ. Res.*, **15**,2, 123–7.

PARKER, J.R. (1969). 'Improving self-images through programming techniques', *Remedial Educ.*, **4**, 145–9.

PARMENTER, T.R. (1970). 'Self-concept development of the partially seeing', *The Slow Learning Child,* **17**,3, 178–87.

PAYNE, J., DRUMMOND, A.W. and LUNGHI, M. (1970). 'Changes in the self-concepts of school leavers who participated in an Arctic expedition', *Brit. J. Educ. Psychol.*, **40**, 211–6.

PEDERSEN, E. (1966). Student characteristics and the impact of the perceived teacher-evaluation on the level of educational aspiration of adolescents. Unpublished Ed.D. dissertation, Harvard University.

PERKINS, H.V. (1958). 'Teachers' and peers' perceptions of children's self-concepts', *Child Developm.*, **29**, 203–20.

PERKINS, H.V. (1958b). 'Factors influencing change in childrens' self-concepts', *Child Developm.*, **29**, 221–30.

PETRAS, J.W. (1968). George Herbert Mead: Essays on his Social Philosophy. New York: Teachers College Press.

PHILLIPS, A.S. (1964). 'The self-concepts of selected groups of training college students in their relation to other variables in the teacher training situation', *Educ. Res.,* **6**,3, 230–4.

PHILLIPS, A.S. (1973). *Adolescence in Jamaica.* London: Macmillan.

PIERS, E.V. and HARRIS, D.B. (1964). 'Age and other correlates of self-concept in children', *J. Educ. Psychol.,* **55**, 91–5.

PONZO, Z. and WRAG STROWIG, R. (1973). 'Relations among sex-role identity and selected intellectual and non-intellectual factors for high school freshmen and seniors', *J. Educ. Res.,* **67**,3, 137–41.

POWERS, J.M. (1971), 'Research note on the self-perception of youth', *Amer. Educ. Res. J.,* **8**, 665–70.

PURKEY, W.W. (1968). 'The search for self: evaluating student self-concepts', Florida Educational Research and Development Council Research Bulletin, University of Florida, **4**,2.

PURKEY, W.W. (1970). Self-Concept and School Achievement. Englewood Cliffs, New Jersey: Prentice-Hall.

QUICKE, J.C. (1975). 'Self-concept and the diagnosis of reading difficulties', *Remedial Educ.,* **2**, 77–81.

QUIMBY, V. (1967). 'Differences in the self-ideal relationships of an achiever group and an underachiever group', *Calif. J. Educ. Res.,* **18**,1, 23–32.

RADLEY, A. (1979). 'The social psychology of learning: a naive description of educational experience', *J. of Further and Higher Educ.,* **3**,1, 82–90.

RATHBONE, H. (1972). 'Examining the open education classroom', *School Rev.,* **80**, 521–49.

RATIGAN, B.J. (1978). A study of students opting for further education at sixteen. Unpublished Ph.D. thesis, Manchester University.

RATIGAN, B.J. (1979). 'Choice of Education at Sixteen', *Oxford Review of Education,* **5**, 1, 41–53.

REICH, A. (1960). 'Pathologic forms of self-esteem regulation', *Psychoanalytic Study of the Child,* **15**, 215–32.

REMANIS, G. (1964). 'Disparity theory and achievement motivation', *J. Abnorm. and Soc. Psychol.,* **69**, 206–10.

RICHER, R.L. (1968). 'Schooling and the self-concept', *New Era,* **68**, 177–200.

RIVLIN, L.G. (1959). 'Creativity and the self-attitudes and sociability of high school students', *J. Educ. Psychol.*, **50**, 147–52.

ROBINSON, N.M. and ROBINSON, H.B. (1976). *The Mentally Retarded Child.* New York: McGraw-Hill.

ROGERS, C.R. (1951). *Client Centred Therapy.* Boston: Houghton Miflin.

ROGERS, C.R. (1962). 'The interpersonal relationship, the core of guidance', *Harvard Educ. Rev.*, **32**, 4.

ROSENBERG, M. (1963). 'Parental interest and children's self-conceptions', *Sociometry*, **26**, 35–49.

ROSENBERG, M. (1965). *Society and the Adolescent Self-Image.* Princeton: University Press.

ROWAN, J. (1975). 'Exploring the self', *New Behaviour*, (11.9.75) 406–9.

SAMUELS, S.C. (1977). *Enhancing Self-Concept in Early Childhood: Theory and Practice.* New York: Human Sciences.

SCHAEFER, C.E. (1969). 'The self-concept of creative adolescents', *J. of Psychol.*, **72**, 233–42.

SECORD, P.F. and JOURARD, S.M. (1953). 'The appraisal of body cathexis: body cathexis and the self', *J. Consult. Psychol.*, **17**, 343–7.

SHAKESPEARE, R. (1975). *The Psychology of Handicap.* London: Methuen.

SHARP, P. (1970). *Students in Full-Time Courses in Colleges of Further Education.* Schools Council Sixth Form Survey Volume 2. London: Books for Schools.

SHAW, J. (1974). *The Self in Social Work.* London: Routledge & Kegan Paul.

SHAW, M.C. and ALVES, S.J. (1963). 'The self-concept of bright underachieving high school students as revealed by an adjective checklist', *Personnel and Guidance J.*, **42**, 401–3.

SHAW, M.C., EDSON, K. and BELL, H.M. (1960). 'The self-concept of bright underachieving high school students as revealed by an adjective checklist', *Personnel and Guidance J.*, **39**, 193–6.

SILVER, A.W. (1958). The self-concept: its relationship to parental and peer acceptance. Abstract of Ph.D. dissertation, Michigan State University.

SIMMONS, C.V. (1980). A study of the personal and moral values of the fourth year pupils of a comprehensive school. *CORE. Collected Original Resources in Education*, 4, 1, Fiche 12F7.

SIMMONS, R., ROSENBERG, F. and ROSENBERG, M. (1973). 'Disturbance in the self-image at adolescence', *Amer. Sociol. Rev.,* **38**, 553–68.

SIMPSON, R.H. (1966). *Teacher Self-Evaluation.* New York: Macmillan.

SLEE, F.W. (1968). 'The feminine image factor in girls' attitudes to school subjects', *Brit. J. Educ. Psychol.,* **38**, 212–4.

SNYGG, D. and COMBS, A.W. (1949). *Individual Behaviour.* New York: Harper.

SOARES, A.T. and SOARES, L.M. (1969). 'Self-perceptions of culturally disadvantaged children', *Amer. Educ. Res. J.,* **6**,1, 31–45.

SOLLEY, C.M. and STAGNER, R. (1956). 'Effects of magnitude of temporal barriers, type of goal, and perception of self', *J. Exper. Psychol.,* **51**, 62–70.

SPAULDING, R.L. (1963). Achievement, Creativity and self-concept correlates of teacher-pupil transactions in elementary schools. United States Office of Education, Co-op Research Report 1352. Urbana: University of Illinois.

STAFFIERI, J.R. (1972). 'A study of social stereotype of body image in children'. In: BARNARD, H.W. and HUCKINS, W.C. *Exploring Human Development.* Boston: Allyn & Bacon.

STAINES, J.W. (1958). 'The self-picture as a factor in the classroom', *Brit. J. Educ. Psychol.,* **28**, 97–111.

STENNER, A.J. and KATZENMEYER, W.G. (1976). 'Self-concepts, ability and achievement in a sample of sixth grade students', *J. Educ. Res.,* **69**,7, 270–3.

STERN, H.H. (1961). 'A follow-up study of adolescents' views of their personal and vocational future', *Brit. J. Educ. Psychol.,* **31**, 170–82.

ST. JOHN, N.H. (1975). *School desegregation: outcomes for children.* New York: Wiley.

STOLZ, H.R. and STOLZ, L.M. (1944). 'Adolescent problems related to somatic variations'. In: *Adolescence* 43rd Year Book National Society for Study of Education Part I, University of Chicago.

STONE, G.P. (1962). 'Appearance and the self'. In: ROSE, A.M. *Human Behaviour and Social Processes.* London: Routledge & Kegan Paul.

STOREY, A.G. (1967). 'Acceleration, deceleration and self-concept', *Alberta J. of Educ. Res.,* **13**,2, 12–8.

STOREY, A.G. and CLARK, R.B. (1968). 'The self-image and wish patterns of the underachiever', *McGill J. of Educ.*, **3**,1, 56–61.

STRANG, R. (1957). *The Adolescent Views Himself.* New York: McGraw-Hill.

STRATHE, M. and HASH, V. (1979). 'The effect of an alternative school on adolescent self-esteem', *Adolescence,* **14**, 53, 185–9.

SULLIVAN, H.S. (1964). 'Beginnings of the Self-System'. In: SOUTHWELL, E.A. and MERBAUM, M. (Eds) *Personality: readings in theory and research.* Belmont: Wadsworth.

TABA, H. (1955). *School Culture.* Washington, D.C.: American Council on Education.

TANNER, J.M. (1978). *Education and Physical Growth.* London: Hodder & Stoughton.

TAYLOR, C. and COMBS, A.W. (1952). 'Self-acceptance and adjustment', *J. Consult. Psychol.,* **16**, 300–18.

THOMAS, D. (1978). *The Social Psychology of Childhood Disability.* London: Methuen.

THOMAS, J.B. (1971). A study of the self-concepts of pupils in their final year at a streamed junior school. Unpublished M.Ed. dissertation, University of Wales.

THOMAS, J.B. (1971b). 'Leadership in the school', *Educ. for Developm.,* **1**,3, 30–4.

THOMAS, J.B. (1973). *Self-Concept in Psychology and Education.* Slough: NFER.

THOMAS, J.B. (1974). 'The self pictures of children in primary school: some qualitative data', *Froebel J.,* **30**, 31–6.

THOMAS, J.B. (1974b). 'Research notice', *Educ. for Developm.,* **3**, 50–1.

THOMAS, J.B. (1978). 'Self-concept and the teacher of physical education', *Health Educ. J.,* **37**,1, 140–1.

TORSHEN, K. (1971), 'The relationship of classroom evaluation to student self-concepts. In: BLOCK, J.H. (Ed) *Mastery Learning: Theory and Practice.* New York: Holt, Rinehart & Winston.

THOMPSON, B. (1974). 'Self-concepts among secondary school pupils', *Educ. Res.,* **17**,1, 41–7.

THOMSON, P. (1971). Children's views of self-concept. Unpublished small scale research, Redland College, Bristol.

TRENT, R.D. (1957). The relation between expressed self-acceptance and expressed attitudes towards negroes and whites among negro children, *J. Genetic Psychol.,* **91**, 25–31.

TREZIZE, R.L. (1967). A descriptive study of the life styles of a group of creative adolescents, *Dissertation Abstracts,* 27-9A, 2754–5.

TROWBRIDGE, N. (1972). 'Self-concept and socio-economic status in elementary school children', *Amer. Educ. Res. J.,* **9**,4, 525–38.

TROWBRIDGE, N. (1973). 'Teacher self-concept and teaching style'. In: CHANAN, G. (Ed) *Towards a science of teaching.* Slough: NFER.

TURNER, R.H. and VANDERLIPPE, R.H. (1958). Self-ideal congruence as an index of maladjustment', *J. Abnorm. Psychol.,* **57**, 203–6.

VENESS, T. (1962). *School Leavers: their aspirations and expectations.* London: Methuen.

VERNON, P.E. (1964). *Personality Assessment: a Critical Survey.* London: Methuen.

VONK, H.G. (1971). 'The relationship of teacher effectiveness to perception of self and teaching purposes', *Dissertation Abstracts,* **31**, 2A, 5862.

WALBERG, H.M. (1967). 'Religious differences in cognitive associations and self-concept in prospective teachers', *J. Soc. Psychol.,* **73**, 83–96.

WALL, W.D. (1968). *Adolescents in school and society.* Slough: NFER.

WALL, W.D. (1977). *Constructive Education for Adolescents.* London: Harrap.

WALKER, D.K. (1973). *Socio-emotional measures for pre-school and kindergarten children.* San Francisco: Jossey-Bass.

WARBURTON, F.W. (1962). 'The measurement of personality', *Educ. Res.,* **4**, 193–205.

WARNOCK REPORT (1978). *Special Education Needs: report of the committee of enquiry into the education of handicapped children and young people.* London: HMSO.

WASHBURN, W.C. (1961). 'Factors associated with levels of self-conceptualization in high school students', *Calif. J. Educ. Res.,* **12**,5, 200–7.

WASHBURN, W.C. (1962). 'Patterns of protective attitudes in relation to differences in self-evaluation and anxiety level amongst high school students', *Calif. J. Educ. Res.,* **12**,2, 84–94.

WEBSTER, M. and SOBIESBZEK, B. (1974). Sources of self-evaluation. New York: Wiley.

WEIDMAN, J.C., PHELAN, W.T. and SULLIVAN, M.A. (1972). 'The influence of educational attainment on self-evaluation of competence', *Sociol. of Educ.,* **45**, 303–12.

WEINREICH, P. (1978). 'Sex and ethnic differences in adolescent self-concept development', *Bull. Brit. Psychol. Soc.,* **31,** 418.

WEINREICH, P. (1979). 'Cross-ethnic identification and self-rejection in a Black Adolescent. In: VERMA, G.K. and BAGLEY, C. (Eds) *Race, Education, and Identity.* London: Macmillan.

WELLS, L.E. and MARWELL, G. (1976). *Self-Esteem: its conceptualization and measurement.* London: Sage.

WENDLAND, M.M. (1967). Self-concept in southern Negro and white adolescents as related to rural-urban residence. Unpublished Ph.D. dissertation, Chapel Hill, University of North Carolina.

WESSMAN, A.E. and RICKS, D.F. (1966). *Mood and Personality.* New York: Holt, Rinehart & Winston.

WHITING, H.T.A. (1973). 'The Body Concept'. In: WHITING, H.T.A. (Ed) *Personality and Performance in Physical Education and Sport.* London: Henry Kimpton.

WILLIAMS, P. (1977). *Children and Psychologists.* London: Hodder & Stoughton.

WISEMAN, S. (1973). 'The educational obstacle race: factors that hinder pupil progress', *Educ. Res.,* **15**,2, 87–93.

WOLF, E.S. (1976). 'Recent advances in the psychology of the self: an outline of basic concepts', *Comprehensive Psychiatry,* **17,** 37–46.

WOLF, E.S., GEDO, J.E. and TERMAN, D. (1972). 'On the adolescent process as a transformation of self', *J. of Youth and Adolescence* 1, 257–72.

WOLFF, S. (1969). *Children under Stress.* Harmondsworth: Penguin.

WOODS, P. (1979). *The Divided School.* London: Routledge & Kegan Paul.

WOOSTER, A.D. and HARRIS, G. (1972). 'Concepts of self and others in highly mobile service boys', *Educ. Res.,* **14**,3, 195–9.

WRIGHT, B. and TUSKA, S. (1966). 'The nature and origin of feeling feminine', *Brit. J. Soc. Clin. Psychol.,* **5,** 140–9.

WYLIE, R.C. (1961). *The Self Concept.* Lincoln: University of Nebraska Press.

WYLIE, R.C. (1974). *The Self Concept I: a review of methodological considerations and measurement instruments.* Lincoln: University of Nebraska Press.

YARWORTH, J.S. and GAUTHIER, W.J. (1978). 'Relationship of student self-concept and selected personal variables to participation in school activities', *J. of Educ. Psychol.*, **70**,3, 335–44.

YOUNG, T.R. (1972). *New Sources of Self.* Oxford: Pergamon Press.

ZAHRAN, H.A.S. (1967). 'The self-concept in the psychological guidance of adolescents', *Brit. J. Educ. Psychol.*, **37**,2, 225–39.